WAGON-WHEELS

Wagon-Wheels

BY

Jim Phelan

ILLUSTRATED BY

Maurice S. Dodd

GEORGE G. HARRAP & CO. LTD
LONDON TORONTO WELLINGTON SYDNEY

First published 1951
by GEORGE G. HARRAP & CO. LTD
182 High Holborn, London, W.C.1

Dewey Decimal Classification : 397

Composed in Bembo type and printed by Western Printing Services, Ltd,
Bristol. Made in Great Britain

CONTENTS

PREFACE

THE Britain of Shakespeare and Dickens and Sir Walter Scott is known to a hundred million readers, from every land under the sun. Strangers who may have come five thousand miles know how to go in search of Stratford-on-Avon, or Kenilworth Castle, or the Old Curiosity Shop.

In the same way the cities of Britain are already familiar to a vast multitude of readers from far and near. The spires of Oxford, the shipyards of the Clyde, the quaint, incredibly ancient crooked streets of Old London—these need no guide-book, since English literature itself is in large part their story.

But there is another Britain, of which the passing traveller seldom catches more than a wistful glimpse—that of the nomad gipsies. The lonely small camp on the edge of a moor, or the painted caravans halted in a green lane—these were ancient five hundred years before Shakespeare was born. But they are still there.

Centuries of progress have altered the face of Britain since Shakespeare's day. Giant cities have grown, and a vast industrial populace bustles eternally about the factories of Birmingham or the offices of London. But the gipsy tents are still on the fringe of the heath, and the painted wagons still wend slowly, unchanged, along the narrow green lanes.

It is the past—the past, alive and mobile in the middle of the twentieth century. It is as if the books and statues of a museum should move and speak. To *that* Britain there is no guide-book. But the present work may serve as an introduction, so that the stranger may see and hear for himself.

It is good hearing.

JIM PHELAN

SAXMUNDHAM
SUFFOLK

CHAPTER ONE

Lords of the Manor

IN the summer of 1923 Charles Baker, a wagon-dwelling gipsy, was serving a short sentence in Norwich Prison for some minor offence of poaching or trespass. The sentence was almost completed, and Baker had only a few weeks to serve, when he received news that his wife, who was about to have a baby, was ill in their caravan, somewhere near Norwich, alone.

Several influential people pressed for a remission of the sentence. A good deal of publicity was aroused. There were news-items about "Gipsy Baker" and photos of the caravan. It seemed likely that the remaining few weeks of the gaol-sentence would be cancelled.

Then, when Baker was expecting to be released, the official communication arrived. He was to stay and complete his sentence. That night he escaped from his cell and set about scaling the outer wall of the prison.

A warder on patrol tackled the escaping prisoner, as was his duty. Baker left him unconscious, managed to cross the prison wall, and got clear away.

The hue and cry followed him over Norfolk and into Lincolnshire. Again there were news-paragraphs about "Gipsy

Baker," more serious now because the wounded warder was at death's door.

Day after day reports came, from places hundreds of miles apart, that the hunted man had been seen. Through the Midlands and over into Cheshire the pursuit followed. Then for a few days all trace of Baker was lost, but presently the hue and cry was hot after him again, into Lancashire.

In 1923 I was myself in Lancashire, with even better reason than Baker to avoid the police. I had been in 'the I.R.A. troubles' in Ireland, and in some variegated 'troubles' of my own besides. It was the most fantastic irony that one day I was tackled in the street and captured, not as Jim Phelan the Irish Republican, but as Gipsy Baker the escaped convict.

Naturally, I kept silent. There was nothing chivalrous about it—if only the police could go *on* thinking I was Gipsy Baker I should have been perfectly happy! So for a while there was other news: "Gipsy Baker captured in Lancashire." One can imagine the feelings of the real man if he had seen a newspaper.

Of course, the police found out almost at once. (Which was nearly the end of Jim Phelan, but that is another story.) Some time afterwards Baker himself was captured, and had a long sentence of penal servitude, as the wounded warder had been all but killed. Baker went to Dartmoor.

Years later I met him, and we had many a laugh at our own expense. The story really was rather a funny one by that time —of my *hoping* to be fetched back to Norwich Gaol as an escaped gipsy convict. Then I lost sight of Baker for a long time.

Twenty-seven years after the Norwich escape, in the spring of 1950, I was talking with an old gipsy by his camp-fire in an East Anglian lane. Ten or twelve members of the family sat by the fire working, while the leader and I talked. A small girl of about five watched us both, and listened to every word.

I wanted to get in touch with Baker if he was alive, and I gave his description, with the first names of himself and his wife. But I used the name Wallace Baker, which was the one generally used. A brown-faced young fellow with curly black hair looked up from his work by the fire.

"It's Charlie Baker you mean," he stated. "And you're Jim Phelan. They plucked you instead of Charlie at Liverpool in 1923. You were willing to face the Norwich charge because you were on the run yourself. Good luck, Jim Phelan from Tipperary."

An instant later the small girl repeated, "Good luck, Jim Phelan. Tipperary."

The boy was speaking of events that occurred many years before he was born. But he had every detail correct, and he knew me at once. It was an eerie experience to hear him speak as if he were reading my history from a printed book.

Of people like that boy, who learnt the 'say' as an infant and never forgot a detail—of such people this book is written.

In earlier years I had met gipsies who knew the story, in places as far apart as Bodmin Moor in Cornwall and the Pass of Killiecrankie in Scotland. Partly because the 'say' had gone so far afield, I met with great friendship and confidence among the wagon-folk.

There were other reasons. For instance, I never go near a gipsy fire in Kent or Cumberland without telling *first* that my mother's name was Collins.

But in all the years I have never ceased to be surprised when I hear by a lonely camp-fire the Baker-Phelan story told by some person who cannot read, who lives hundreds of miles from Norwich, and who was still unborn when the incidents occurred.

That is tradition.

We talk and write much about the power of tradition, but few opportunities occur to see the thing working. In a modern industrial civilization like that of Britain or the United States tradition counts for little or nothing.

That may be a good thing or a bad—who can say? But so many cases are on record in which tradition has been right when the world's scholars were wrong that it is thoroughly fascinating to see it at work. By far the best example in these islands is among the wagon-dwellers.

It would be well if readers, as well as my romani friends, were to note that I refer to 'wagon-dwellers,' and do not use the term 'gipsies.' Gipsy tradition will come best from a romani scholar—or from an old woman giving a say. The general traditions, going back many hundreds of years, are shared by all the caravan-folk, of whatever origin.

Scots and Irish people, at any rate until recently, passed on their traditions as the wagon-dwellers do, as the sagas of the Norsemen were passed on. A child learns the stories by rote, perhaps not differentiating them from fairy tales, then year by year comes to separate the characters as real people. The little girl by the fire in East Anglia would be learning the Baker-Phelan story almost as soon as I had left the camp.

Inevitably with such a method of transmitting history there is telescoping of time and place. Two cases occur to me, both very much to the point.

In the summer of 1939 the police at Bledlow, near High Wycombe in Buckinghamshire, had the utmost difficulty in separating two families of caravan-people, who fought with fists and bludgeons and other weapons.

Locally the affair was dismissed as a tinkers' fight. In fact the Cannadines had attacked the Herons because the Heron family had beaten Toby Cannadine to death with bludgeons on the common after Woking Fair.

Furthermore, some of the Herons admitted the offence, after the police had left.

But no person named Cannadine had been reported killed. Besides which, Woking Fair has not been held for nearly a hundred years.

The second example of telescoping is even more curious. One evening I talked with Sam Scampe, the chief of a wagon-clan in Suffolk. We were discussing a last-minute reprieve which had occurred after some sensational murder-case, and

Sam told me sadly the tragedy in his own family. Every one round the fire knew the story.

Sam's grandfather was arrested one evening near Stow-on-the-Wold, after a fair. (There were details about his clothes, and the amount of money he carried with him; also a description of a knife known as a family heirloom.) Scampe was charged with murder, was tried almost at once. The evidence was conclusive, he was sentenced to death, and was duly hanged. Immediately after his execution a reprieve arrived, accompanied by proof of his innocence.

It was a moving story, told there in the flicker of the wood-fire, among the caravans. Perhaps the most impressive feature was the manner in which one or other of those who lay by the fireside would now and then furnish a detail or fill a pause with a mimed quotation. But—when I checked the dates and places I found that Sam Scampe's grandfather could not possibly have been hanged as described—had, in fact, died in a caravan at Lockerbie in Scotland.

Then in January 1950 I had a recurrence of the eerie feeling that came when the gipsy youngster called out my name and history. Switching on the radio, I heard a programme describing the execution of Sam Scampe, exactly as I had heard it described in Suffolk.

There was no possibility of doubt. The radio-writer had done his work thoroughly, had searched the records and unearthed the facts. Only it was Sam Scampe's great-great-grandfather, and he was hanged in 1840. Just as Toby Canna-dine was in fact bludgeoned to death by the Herons after Woking Fair—in the year 1809.

Those two examples show the chief pitfall of traditional history. The word father or grandfather creeps into a say, and is passed on. Such cases are few, and are easily corrected if necessary.

Generally it is unnecessary. Because in all the more important says, such as those concerning lineage, territorial division, or the bequest of property, several women share the say, and it is checked every year. In that way major errors are eliminated.

Thus in a hundred years or so some youngster by a campfire may tell that one Charles Baker and one Jim Phelan broke out of (or into) Norwich Gaol in the year 1963, thus missing the point by a whole generation. Such says are unimportant, and will vary from decade to decade.

But it is in the highest degree unlikely that, at the same campfire a hundred years hence, there will be any confusion as to where the territory of the Smiths from Hertfordshire ends and that of the Taylors from Bedfordshire begins. Half a dozen old women, of different families, will be there to quote it, syllable for syllable, verbatim.

In civilization personal stories are forgotten or distorted, but treaties and contracts are filed in the archives. It is the same thing.

Most of the wagon-people read no books or newspapers. There is no question of stupidity or ignorance. Merely the accomplishment is unnecessary, belonging to a way of life other than their own. Few city-dwellers can follow the tracks of a lost horse, or read the signs of wild life in a hedgerow! Why should they?

With no written or printed records, the wagon people live entirely by tradition. It would be pleasant if readers understood this, because then it will be easy to grasp one fact which underlies the whole culture of the wagon-dwellers in Britain, and which forms the main thread of this book. It can be stated very simply, but might be startling if the existence of wagon tradition were forgotten or ignored. It is that the land of England, with much of Scotland and Ireland as well, is divided and held and owned by two separate and distinct groups of owners, dwelling side by side—the proprietors recognized by law and the wagon-dwelling people often described as gipsies.

There is nothing quite like it in the rest of nature. It is not a mere parasitism like that of the orchid or mistletoe. In those cases, if the host plant dies the parasite plant dies too. But there is not the slightest doubt that, if our civilization came to an end to-morrow, the land of Britain would still be owned and used by roughly the same number of wagon-people, few more and few less.

When a gipsy caravan rumbles along an English lane it appears to be heading into the unknown, into the obscurity and chaos of the wild. In fact, its route is fixed as inexorably as that of an express train. A barrow-boy from the East End of London, attempting to enter the residence of Lord Rothschild, would have roughly the same chance as a Scampe caravan from Suffolk heading, uninvited, for a camp-ground in the territory of the Norfolk Bakers or the Colins of Kent.

Even that parallel is not sufficiently strong. The nearest analogy is that of a Soviet warship coming unannounced to anchor in Portsmouth Harbour!

Once that fact of territorial division is grasped the story of the wagon-folk becomes comprehensible. Without understanding of that division, and of the traditional method in which it is kept on record, every attempt at a narrative fritters away into vapid and puerile romance or sterile scholasticism.

Cast back to the early sixteenth century, and the thing becomes plain. At that time the land of England—and of the less wild parts of Scotland—was divided among civilized people roughly as it is divided among the wagon-folk to-day.

The Yorkshireman who travelled in Hampshire—without a pass—did so at his peril. The villager who went even a few miles into an adjacent county—without a pass—had a story to tell for the rest of his life. The records exist, in thousands, are well known to historians, and are fascinating for us nowadays.

Times changed. Civilization spread. Commerce waxed, and industrialism was born. The power of the big families decreased, and gradually the borders were overrun. Between city and city there was right of way. The English world was now one of bricks and mortar. Civilization had triumphed.

It never touched the wagon-dwellers. Their culture, and their division of territory, is still pre-Elizabethan.

Sam Scampe and all his tribe were involved in a bad road-accident at Washbrook, near Ipswich, in the winter of 1949. Of five wagons, two were smashed. One boy was killed, two horses wounded to uselessness.

It was December when they could move again, with three wagons only and with no town or village in which they could winter. They kept on the road, in Suffolk.

To the romantic they were a picturesque tribe of gipsies travelling the wild, free countryside, with all the world before them, at liberty to go whither they would, onward, ever onward on the broad highway. To those who have come thus far along the road with me they will not appear in that light.

They kept to the lanes of Suffolk, because Suffolk is the Scampe country. North were the Bakers of Norfolk, with exactly as many people as Norfolk will support. West were the Smiths in Hertfordshire, with as many people as their country can maintain. South were the Brants of Essex, and over the river were the Colins in Kent—each with as many persons as their territory would support.

It was a hard winter. With three wagons instead of five, and with two horses dead, impoverished and crowded as they were, the Scampes found it harder still. However, they survived—but it was in the lanes of Suffolk and nowhere else. Because Suffolk is their own country.

Cast back again to the sixteenth century, or even to the seventeenth, when the Plague was in London. Who cared, in Salisbury, for instance, except to lock their gates against intruders?

From those days, with few and unimportant accretions from the intervening stages of civilization, dates the culture of the people who live above wagon-wheels. The things that have happened in the cities since about 1500 mean nothing to them.[1]

---

[1] Include printing, democracy, and the Reformation as well as slum-life, unemployment, and sex-crime.

The land of this country is still apportioned among the families as it was in the days of York and Lancaster.

Sam Scampe had only three wagons instead of five, and it was December. But he led his people, zigzag in the lanes, wherever there was a patch of grass or a running stream, a promising camp-ground or a hospitable landowner, and always in Suffolk, until the winter was past.

Always in Suffolk. Where else could he lead them?

When one understands his reasons, his compulsions, the story of the wagons, of the culture that goes on wheels, will also be easy to understand. It is in fact a story uncommonly like the history of what was happening in England or France a few hundred years ago. Only the wagon-wheels are still going the road to-day.

CHAPTER TWO

The Say of the Seven Cannadine

ON a disused and grass-grown road near Hemel Hempstead I talked one day with a young and exceptionally intelligent wagon-man. Since Hemel Hempstead is in Hertfordshire, no one who has read the first chapter will need to be told that the travelling man's name was Henry Smith.

It was necessary that I should get in touch with Henry a few days later. But I was on my way to London, while he would be moving on that afternoon.

Picking a village through which he would pass, I said I would wire him at the post-office there, and asked if he could read. He shook his head, with a tolerant smile.

"Not that I object, brother," he conceded. "I don't think print-reading does people any real harm. I *don't*," he insisted.

A professional writer, priding myself on some small dexterity in the use of words, I was being told, almost in a pitying tone, that my activities, and the whole vast power of the Press, were not actually *injurious* to mankind. Worse still, I felt somehow guilty, and stammered a few words to the effect that print-and-paper juggling was my job.

Then I rallied, and tried to score a point. How, I inquired, if reading and writing were superfluous, was I ever to get in touch with him again? How was I to send a message, and some money I owed him?

"Oh, that," Smith told me carelessly. "Give it to one of our people in Watford."

I explained that I was unlikely to be in Watford. Also that in any case it was a very big town, and I might inquire for days before finding a man named Smith!

"Edgware?" he asked. "Or Barnet? Is that near enough to London?" When I said yes he nodded to a tall, spindly wheeled gig and a low, light four-wheeled trolley near his caravan in the lane. Then he grinned, tolerantly still.

"If you saw one like that," he inquired, "outside a pub or a junk-store in Barnet or Edgware—would you think it belonged to a writing man, yes?"

I was sensible enough to say no more. Two days later I gave the message to a man I had never previously seen, by a tall gig outside a rag-shop in Barnet. It was an important message—meant the saving of perhaps forty pounds to me in the purchase of a caravan—but I handed it over, blindly, as instructed. A week afterwards, when I met Black Harry Smith in Hatfield, my message had been delivered and my business had been completed.

That personal and individual approach to affairs seems fantastically outmoded and inefficient at first glance. Is Lord Beaverbrook, for instance, to know the home and habits of every *Daily Express* reader! Can the building of a two-million-pound battleship, or negotiation for the sale of an oilfield, be arranged by the sending of a personal message to Tom, Dick, or Harry?

In those last four words—tradition be praised—lies the clue. The overwhelming majority of civilized communications are quite unimportant. But every vital decision, every matter of

B

top-rank urgency, both in commerce and politics, is in fact settled after a personal message from Tom to Dick, or from Harry to both.

The Smiths of Hertfordshire have a wide range, overlapping the Middlesex border and touching the edges of Bucks. Anywhere from Watford, near London, to the environs of Cambridge there will be a Smith in a caravan, or on a high-wheeled dogcart, or driving a fast flat trolley. From market town to market town, and from fair to fair, while going about their other business, they carry messages by word of mouth, about the affairs of their own people and their own territory.

A kind of local government, in other words.

Transmission of a say about the Scampe family's accident near Ipswich, or about the tangle of identities between Charles Baker and myself, would have no place on the Smith network. It is interesting to inquire how such a message can get from Cumberland to Cornwall. Few outsiders besides myself are allowed to know anything about it.

Which is fair enough. Few wagon-people besides myself are allowed into the offices of Reuter's or the Press Association. It is the same thing. The simplest comparison is with the feature pages of a daily or Sunday newspaper, where entertainment value is opposed to news-content. The gig-and-trolley messengers are strictly business, functioning every day up and down the country. Entertainment stories are only passed on at intervals, where many families are gathered after a big fair or before a race-meeting. At such a time the old women give the say to one another for hours at a time by the camp-fires.

Editors and journalists, publishers and novelists of the unwritten word, they recite their stories on Epsom Downs, at Aintree Racecourse or Newmarket Heath, or on the fringe of Barnet Fair. Small girls listen—generally the brightest one of each family being chosen for encouragement. In civilization the young writers are supposed to be encouraged in the same way.

Contrast two facets of the Baker story. In the first hours and days after Charlie's escape the wagon-men would relay the story swiftly from market to market. Baker was one of their own people. The story was 'front-page news,' as we put it. The messages would not necessarily ask anyone to help Baker on his way, but—he was one of the wagon-people, and he was hunted.

Over from Norwich into King's Lynn the message would go, verbally, within a couple of hours: "Charlie Baker. Broke Norwich Gaol. He may come to your fire." Across to Sleaford and on into Lincoln that say would still be passed, although by a different family, then up to Doncaster and across to Sheffield, out to Stockport and on for Manchester: "One of the Norfolk Bakers. Broke Norwich Gaol. May come to your fire."

Different families, who knew little of the Bakers except that they owned Norfolk, would still pass the say in haste, on to Bolton, and up through North Lancs to the Scottish border: "Baker from Norfolk. Broke gaol. May come to your fire."

The daily papers may and may not have been ahead of the wagon-people's say, in places like Bristol and Cardiff. But the odds are in favour of the gigs and trolleys—along the route that might be taken by Charlie Baker. Hot news!

The later and longer story, about the mix-up between Charles and myself, would travel in no such haste. That say would be a matter of singsong narrative, from an old woman of the Bakers, perhaps by a fire at the Goose Fair of Nottingham, telling her say to the Burdocks and Cleavers. Some woman of the other family would memorize it, and thereafter it would spread, county by county, at race-meeting or fair.

First thought of any civilized person is—what a cumbrous form of entertainment! But it all depends on what you call things.

In civilization three-sevenths of our income and energy are spent in paying for wars past and future, and in written or printed discussion of such payment. Nearly two-sevenths are spent in advertising and publicity of one kind and another. About one-seventh goes in producing and writing about food and similar things. The other seventh goes in religion and art, stories and films—in culture, briefly.

The wagon-people expend no wealth on war or publicity. About six-sevenths of their time and energy are spent in getting about, and in the business of living. The other seventh goes in culture, as in our own case. But they have no films, novels, sculpture, religious writings, or pictorial art—just stories. On balance they seem to fare even better than we do.

War and advertising do really occupy most of our printed pages. Black Harry Smith, who has never lived one night under a roof, is of opinion that such activities do no real harm!

He made one other statement—a flat and staggering contradiction of everything that has been written by scholars and philosophers for centuries past. It is a commonplace that war is the great pruner, the chief check on over-population. If men did not engage in destructive wars this world would be filled by a teeming, happy populace. Or by an overcrowded and miserable populace—according to the views of the expounding philosopher.

Black Harry says casually that house-people spend most of their time and money on making wars and killing one another, and that *therefore* they get "far too many; far too many for the roads to hold." The statement appears ridiculously false until one starts to count.

Wagon-dwelling population in England has remained about the same since Tudor times. The population of the civilized war-making world has doubled or trebled. Since World Wars came into fashion, with slaughter of millions as a commonplace, world population has increased at a terrifying rate.

Pacifist philosophers, claiming that the human race is rapidly being wiped out by war, might do well to talk with Black Harry Smith. On the other hand, the bellicose philosophers, proudly asserting that war is the great beneficent pruner, might likewise consider Black Harry's curt dogma.

But perhaps the old women giving the say about love and marriage, about horse-trading and road-lore, giving the say about good and bad luck, omitting the three-sevenths war-talk and the two-sevenths publicity, are not in need of our pity after all. Now when I give a say, here and there through this book, no print-reader will be impatient if it is about simple things, about men and women or horses and roads, with no mention of civilized subjects like manpower and defence estimates, refrigerators and contango, vacuum-cleaners, theosophy, diamond tiaras, and cheap margarine.

Here is an old woman of the Cannadine, giving a say by a fire at Small Heath, near Birmingham. There is a circle of listeners from other families, because there has been a big fair and the wagons have halted for several days. At the feet of the ancient woman a small girl sits, now and then repeating the phrases noiselessly, as do some of the adults in the circle.

No harm they mean, the old woman repeats again and again, the gorgia mean no harm when they take our land and build their house-towns where all must keep in off the roads. Aye, all.

A strange belief, that people should stay in house-towns, and never see the road again, never again till they die. A strange belief, but the gorgia mean no harm, and do no harm. For what can it matter if they give their say on bits of paper with words, and the words tell the gorgia people where to come and go, but make no matter to people on the road, of course.

Now, the housemen's papers will put you in mind of the Say of the Seven Cannadine. For the housemen have papers with words on for every call. Some when a girl marries, and all will have seen them. Others when a chavo is born, so that the gorgia men will know where every chavo is in the towns. But that's for people in houses, of course, and not for people on the road, so it did no harm, for long and long.

Only now it came on that there was a war. Something about a Kaiser, I think they called him, from Germany, where the Brants of Essex used to live long ago. The Kaiser, from Germany. It was to be a big war, that was sure, and the gorgia went in ships and trains and wagons, by hundreds and thousands and thousands more, to fight the Kaiser.

Now it came on that at first this was good. For travelling people, I mean. Soldiers by thousands in camps on every road, laughing and generous and quick on the give, for the wagon-folk. Navvies and factory-men by thousands more, making the things for the fight with the Kaiser, earning big money and quick on the give as well, when a wagon came the road. Aye, it was good at first.

And there was tatting.

No one ever before saw such tatting as there was for that war with the Kaiser from Germany. Before that if a wagon-family made a tatting, and ran down a big fire with tins and kettles, to collect the tin melted out of them, then they might work a week and have twenty gold pounds at the end for the ingot of tin.

But when the Kaiser war came the tatting-money jumped high. Something the gorgia people do with the tin when there is a war, making bullets or the like. So now the tatting gave plenty of money, and those were good days for the travelling people. For a year or two.

But the gorgia had been fighting all this time. So now the housemen in the Kaiser's country had few more men. And the gorgia over this side had few more men either. They gave a say about it, and this was their say. Every young man must go to the war. Unless he had a paper to prove he was unfit.

The paper would be to stop the young housemen who wanted to hide and not go to the fighting. So that was the say—if the young man had no paper he must go to the war.

Now that, for the travelling people, was not so good as the generous soldiers and the big money for the tin. No.

Well, there would be eighteen wagons of the Cannadine on the road that year, or nineteen, counting one broke at the fork above Gretna Green. Nineteen wagons, with my sons

and grandsons and great-grandsons in them, the tall Cannadine, the tawny tall Cannadine of the Border. Aye.

Seven of them were the right age, the right age where they
had to have a paper, or go to the fighting, or go to the gaol.
Seven tall Cannadine, that would fight on the drop of a hat,
battle a man on a fairground for a sovereign, or the half of a
sovereign, or sixpence, or a cigarette. But not wanting battles
with bullets against Kaisers, of course, just on some houseman's
say.

Only *there* was the hole in the road, *there* was the flood at
the ford. They should have a paper, or go to the war. It was
the say. And they had no papers. For of all the young
housemen they only gave papers to sickly ones or crippled.
And how could the seven tall fighting Cannadine get sickly
papers? Not they.

It came to the summer-end talk, down here at Small Heath
after the Fair, that year in the beginning of the paper-say. And
of all the wagon-people there was no young man but must go
to the Kaiser war, since all were the age and all were fighting
healthy. So none had a paper.

There was a long say that night, here by the fires. Most of
the boys were for going to the war, and be done with it. And
some few thought they might get away to the wild parts of
the country, and keep out. But the seven Cannadine would
have neither of those things.

They would not go to the housemen's war, they said, because they knew nothing about that quarrel. But neither
were they to skulk away in the wilds. Then no one knew
what they *would* do, for papers they had none, and not likely
to have.

They settled it that night, after the rest of the wagon-people
had gone, and the heart in me screamed like a broken-leg foal
when I heard their say. Seven of them, they sat by the fire and
played cards, to see which one would lose the hand.

Young, handsome Black Simon Cannadine lost, Simon that
could box a champion, with the straight left fist that was known

at every fair from Barnet to Dundee. Simon with the straight left, he lost, and he went to the housemen's war.

He got no papers of course. Not he. But a suit of soldier's clothes, with straps and things on him. Then soon they gave him leave for a week to go home and see his family. So he came back for a talk, back to the wagons.

Over near Gloucester we were camped, on the night when it was time for Simon to go back from his leave. They had the rest of the say that night, him and his six brothers and cousins, to finish what they had begun at the card-playing. Seven of them, tall and healthy, the downy fighting Cannadine, with the black curls hanging over their hard, laughing faces, that even their own mother would be hard put to tell one from another.

But soon there was a difference. And soon you would know one from the rest. Aye.

Connie Cannadine, Simon's brother, fetched the long-handled axe, and in one chop he took the left hand from Simon, just where the thumb finished. The good left hand of Black Simon Cannadine, that he lost playing cards at Small Heath. Then they tied a wire round the stump, to keep him from dying of the blood-stream, and he took his road back to the gorgia soldiers.

Not for weeks did we see him again, after being in the soldier's gaol while they tried to prove it was lies about his hand being cut off in a machine. But how could they? So they let him go, because they wanted no single-wing ducks on that war-flight of theirs. No. The stump was better by that time, so he laughed when he came back. And a paper they gave him, with words on it in print, to say he must go to no war. But only for one, only for Simon Cannadine, and the paper had Simon's name on.

Well, it was but a short time until they came for Dan, and now it was his turn to go to the war. Nor it wasn't long before Dan was home on seven days' leave, back by the wagons, in soldiers' clothes and with straps on him like Simon had. Then soon it was the night before he was to go back to the soldiers, and then Connie got out the big axe again.

Thin as a bee's wing would be the slice he chopped from Simon's stump, the stump of his fine left arm, and tied a wire round it to stop him from dying of the blood-stream. Then away back to the soldiers went tall Dan Cannadine, with one hand and a stump tied with wire. Only, of course, it was Simon, in the soldiers' clothes and with Dan's soldier-papers.

Six weeks passed before he was back, sickly-looking because he had been in the gaol and in the gorgia hospital. But with his paper. His good second paper. In the name of Dan Cannadine. Aye.

Little rest he got, poor Simon. For the stump was not long better when they took Nathan for the housemen's war, and then in another month Nathan came on leave in the soldiers' clothes. And Connie got out the axe, to slash another thin slice from the end of Simon's stump, and send him away to the soldiers in Nathan's clothes and with Nathan's papers.

So it went on, and so all went well. For all the tall Cannadine had papers, to show in the printed words that they must not go to the war. A great world is the gorgia house-world, with papers for all, to give the say and to tell who must come and go.

A dollcie kushti burra world it is, and fair, always fair. For indeed it was a fair dicker, to swop one left hand for seven good papers. Always the word-papers have their use. And the gorgia do no harm.

CHAPTER THREE

Tawny Charlie

THE say of the seven Cannadine, a simple story of impersonation to avoid conscript-service, has few unusual features. Newspaper files, and police-court records, can furnish ample evidence that, at the time of which the story is told, the wagon-people had no monopoly of any such technique.

Only in the direct, savage efficiency of the method adopted, and in the fact that there were six impersonations instead of one or two, does the say of the seven Cannadine merit attention. Opportunity for six consecutive impersonations can occur in few communities.

But all sheep look alike except to a shepherd, and all Chinese are the same in Occidental eyes. In the same way any seven wagon-men of about the same age, especially if related—as they will be—look alike to a civilized person.

That principle is explained, dramatically and in startling fashion, in the old woman's say about Black Simon Cannadine. But it is applied, in a less spectacular manner, a thousand times a day and as a matter of course, in the wagon way of life.

My friends on the road will not mind my writing this chapter. There is no giving away of secrets, no harm in telling about it now. Times have changed. The switch of identities was chiefly necessary in the business of tatting, and it is no longer essential.

Tatting is a mainstay occupation with many families who live in wagons. People with names like Smelter, Smith, Tinker, Brazier, and so on really are named after their present or recent occupations. In civilization there is no reason to suppose that a man called Rank should stink a little, or that a lawyer named Crook is dishonest. But where one meets a wagon-man called Tinker or Smith it is very long odds that he is a tinsmith or 'does a bit of tatting.'

Tatting generally means the salvage of scrap tin. The rewards fluctuate. Before the 1914 War tin was about £35 a ton in the crude ingot. The wagon-people did not concentrate on tatting up to then. But within a few years, during the First World War, the price jumped to £90 a ton. Then it fell away again for a while.

Thereafter the price rose and fell, and the wagon-people's interest in tatting (as against the manufacture of heather-brooms, say) rose and fell accordingly. During the Second World War the price soared, and again dropped with the return of peace. But in early 1950 tin was £700 a ton, and tatting was back with a vengeance.

It would seem at first sight that everything was perfectly simple. The tinkers and other wagon-folk have a well-established technique for the recovery of block tin, from the old tins thrown away on every city dump. Since tin was in urgent demand, one might have expected that the tatting would have gone forward without interruption.

In practice things are not so simple. To begin with, the wagon-families move about, take turns at the 'pitches.' Thus they avoid trouble with the police and obey their own tribal laws at the same time.

Consider the wagon-law first. Pitches vary in value. One

pitch may yield five rabbits, one pheasant, seven shillings in coppers, a few bundles of rags, and a small load of scrap-iron, perhaps from two villages or three. The potentialities of every pitch from Plymouth to Cape Wrath are known and kept on record in the say.

Ten miles off, near a big city dump, another pitch may yield tins and more tins, ample firewood, space for the big run-down fire, eventually a tin ingot worth a hundred pounds. In the same period of time that the first pitch takes to furnish seven shillings and five rabbits.

Where all the people in a territory are of the same clan—as they will be—family and tribal law indicates a circling of the caravans. The pitches are held for less than a week, and a tatting run-down occupies about six days.

There is another sidelight. The police in most districts only permit caravan people to stay for three days, not six. (Thereafter it is a case of attempted squatting, and trespass.) Actually the period named, in most cases, is one full day, but by an admirable casuistry it works out to nearly three. A wagon pulls in at dawn on Tuesday morning, pulls out at sundown on Thursday night—has only been on the pitch for one full day, Wednesday.

Many readers will already be familiar with the basic technique of tatting. (There has been a book about it, and I described the process at some length in a couple of magazine articles.) On a corrugated-iron floor a huge bonfire is built, with alternate layers of wood and old tins. When the fire is lighted molten tin runs down the grooves of the corrugated-iron, flows into a hollow to form an ingot.

But it takes time to collect and place the firewood, more time to collect and place the tins. The legal period of "one full day" would mean waste of labour, waste of time, fighting about tins and firewood and ingots. Chaos, in fact.

So much for the application of city law.

In the tinkers' own law there are two solutions to the problem. The first is where pairs of tatting-groups work together.

One lot of caravans pull in on a pitch, its people work three days on the tins and the firewood; then they pull out and get along to the next pitch. Their opposite numbers pull in immediately afterwards, complete the bonfire, make the run-down, and divide the price of the ingot.

It does not always work well. City merchants, business-men in general, have no monopoly of commercial scepticism. Some-times there are fights about the size or alleged size of the tat.

The other way is simpler, and straight wagon-way thinking. Gabriel Cannadine, with his wagons and his family, arrives at a tatting-pitch, and they work for three days. In a district where the police are obstructive Gabriel Cannadine and his family will have departed at sundown on the third day, and Nathaniel Wallace Baker will have moved in with his own wagons.

Only, of course—as the old woman giving the say might put it—of course it is Gabriel all the time, with Nat's house-papers, and all sheep look alike except to a shepherd. The papers are in order, the police are satisfied, and so are the wagon-folk.

The other, and formerly the chief, reason for constant impersonation and resultant general anonymity had its origin in the incredibly savage laws operated against the gipsies since the time of James V of Scotland. A man might be hanged, and often *was* hanged, because his name was Graham or Fay, or because he had black eyes!

The records provide a terrifying study in vicious and sense-less repression.

Hence it was often literally a matter of life and death for a man named Fay to be able to prove that his name was Graham, or vice versa. Tradition is strong, and from those days has been handed down the lore of impersonation. Ask a wagon-man his name on the roadside and immediately, automatically, he will furnish an alias—and be able to prove that the alias is his real name. In many parts of South America the Indians do likewise, and for similar reasons.

Look at a wagon-man's trolley or gig, and on the shaft you will often see the surname put first, as in many European countries. Cooper Hanry or Baker Cherlas may catch a casual eye. On inquiry the man will generally say that he painted the name upside down by accident, and spelt the second word incorrectly, he not being much of a book-scholar!

Adaptability! The adaptability of these my friends from the road, living side by side with the houseman and keeping the letter of his laws, as well as obeying their own more stringent code, is comparable only to that of the robin, adjusting himself in brain and body until he can come straight to a kitchen table, in friendly confidence, while remaining always of the wild. If one thinks of the wagon-people thus it is easy to understand them.

Of course, there is also a simple, necessary, and modern causation for the swift switch of indentities among the road-folk. Here and there a landowner or a farmer may object if a rabbit or two should become soup over a camp-fire. There may be a record that one Phelan (to take a safe name that will offend no one) has been rabbiting. It is, naturally, useful if a suspected person can prove that his name is—something other than Phelan. After a few years, or a few generations, the thing becomes automatic. It is not only interesting but gives something of a thrill to note that these people, the proudest individualists in the world, have almost sunk their personal identities in the blanketing anonymity of the family group.

Perhaps a person of strong character has no real need of a printed document to show that he is himself.

The contrast between civilized law and wagon-law in the matter of fixing a given person's identity is amusing. We concentrate on documents, on names, descriptions, records, and references—as an old wagon-woman put it, we rely on papers copied from other papers. The travelling people have no romani identity-cards or birth-certificates. They merely *know* the person, by his intimate bodily shape, by his family smell, by voice-notes indistinguishable to city ears. It would be easier for a fox to pose as a rabbit than for one gipsy to deceive another about his identity.

One of the most common and normal acts for a wagon-person sending a message a long distance is for him to include the road-equivalent of an identity card, some part of his own body, generally the hair. The story of Dick Coyle occurs to me.

Coyle was a tramp, an ordinary long-distance, foot-slogging vagabond. Not a romani himself, he was known and liked by many romani people, especially in Scotland. Dick once delivered a message from somewhere near Inverness to a gipsy family camped near Plymouth, six hundred miles away. It was an important message, and involved his being given eighty pounds in notes.

A wagon-family far from wealthy were to hand over eighty pounds to a vagrant unknown to them, who was not even a romani, and who had not one written line to justify his story. Naturally, they made inquiries—in their own fashion.

The tramp cleared his throat in a certain way. Then he handed over a curl of black hair. After he had been made to repeat the throat-clearing one or twice, and after the lock of hair had been smelt and *tasted*, the money was handed over.

In good humour at having been found worthy of such trust, Coyle asked in jest what would have happened if he had fetched the lock of hair from a dead man's body. In an instant he was gripped and held by hostile men, while the hair-lock was tested again, by two old women, to prove that its owner was alive and that the tramp was joking.

Elsewhere I have told the story of a girl who, having been absent for a year from her family's wagons, returned with a two-months-old baby. She alleged that she was really married to a romani man, who had gone abroad, and that the child was his, but she had no evidence of any kind except a marriage-certificate.

Naturally, the housemen's paper was worthless, since it proved nothing about the child's parentage. Things looked bad for the putatively erring girl.

Then one old woman sought a girl who had been married to a man of the alleged husband's family, threw the baby's napkin in her face, and the other girl was cleared of suspicion.

There was no doubt. There would be no doubt. Even the most law-abiding and highly civilized suburban mother would have known, in a second. Mothers everywhere know things like that. The rest of us forget.

Now I have taken a long time to get here, to the point where I can say that many or most of the stories we tell in civilization are not stories at all. A staggeringly high percentage of novels and shorter tales, a still higher percentage of film-stories, depend upon misunderstanding between lovers, mistaken identity, cross-purposes, undetected falsehood about love or hatred, impersonation, and sex-ignorance.

There aren't any such things really. Every typist who pays a florin to see a film knows it. Every wagon-child over six years old knows it too. Look back, for instance, at Shakespeare's plots. Again and again the same pitifully thin story crops up, of the girl who pretends she is a man. To her lover! Or to a girl-rival!

No man would or could be deceived—not even in an actor's pub or in a hostelry adjacent to the B.B.C. No girl would be deceived, for the tenth part of a second. But in the cities it is necessary for us to pretend that men do not know the smell of a girl, and that a girl does not know when a man wants to mate with her. For some reason it is necessary for us to pretend that we do not know a colt from a filly.

No casuist, frightened to contemplate healthy men and women, must say that in the pretence lies literary art. Because there is no such pretence in the works of Homer, no such meagre and paltry self-deception in the stories of the Old Testament. And there are no such infant tricks in the stories of the wagon-men.

The tales are all about people or animals *au naturel*, about the forces of nature or of good and bad luck. The million writers (naturally, the present author is as guilty as the rest) who have followed the beaten path of flimsy pretence fare badly when compared with the old women giving the say.

There is one say, very ancient, which I would like to tell, to set its content of trickery against our own feeble pretences, in which story-teller and reader alike have to deceive themselves. The old women tell it by the fires, often as if the events occurred a few years ago, although the story is a factual one, dates from about 1812, and has been checked by Walter Simson, Sir Walter Scott, and others.

Now I will give the say of Tawny Charlie, of handsome Charlie Graham from above the Border, who travelled the roads in Fife and Perth. Taller than most was Charlie, black by the sun and by his mother as well, ringlets hanging dark on his shoulders, and with small feet and hands like a girl that will dance.

Women and horses he knew right well, and women and horses knew Charlie. They would come to him.

It was not just that he had the touch with horses, for many a wagon-man has that. Nor the touch with women alone, for many a man, in towns even, will have the girls to follow him. But Charlie Graham could call or whistle, and up from her bridal bed would leap the high lord's new-made wife, to follow him, or the high lord's favourite mare would come tearing her stable door down, to be off with Tawny Charlie.

A good call and a lifting touch to have, but dangerous at that time, there in that country above the Border, where the housemen's law was steel-trap cruel, where the housemen's law was adder-wicked, against the travelling people. When a travelling man could be hung and dead inside an hour if but two housemen said that he was a travelling man and had black eyes. Tawny Charlie had black eyes, and was a travelling man. But he had the gift with horses and women, and more than that he was liked by men as well. So he was close and clan with the high lord Airlie, the lord of the land above the Border. A houseman.

Many a houseman, of high and low, loved Tawny Charlie

C

Graham, for his laughing ways, and his gift to dance and sing, and the lively, lovely say of his voice. But in talk and toping one night above Perth, with the high lord Airlie and his housemen friends, then Tawny Charlie boasted. Boasted and said he would whistle away the thing Lord Airlie loved best, be it woman or horse or tame black crow.

It was a mad say. Because the high lord Airlie had liquor. And he was to be married next day.

Hot man-blood and hot liquor between them brought the challenge, and Tawny Charlie went out from Perth with the call in his ears that he was a boasting fool. A boasting fool to give a say like that. Unless he could prove it next day.

Then by morning all was forgotten and gone, so that the high lord Airlie and his housemen friends were close and clan with Charlie again, and the handsome dark one with the ringlets must be bade to the wedding, and dance at the bridal, and wish the lord Airlie luck.

It is a short say, the next part, and a dozen songs have been made of it. A very short say it takes to tell that Tawny Charlie whistled and she came.

Now the high lord Airlie drank and swore, and drank again and laughed from his liquor. By the lords of his heaven-house he swore again that Charlie was the master, and the call was a magic and none should harm Charlie Graham.

Nor when the high lady came back to her father's house, in a week or when would it be, there was none to harm her, and all knew that Charlie and the high lord Airlie would be close and clan again whenever they should meet.

As they were when they met, and in liquor they laughed at the power and magic of Charlie's call. So all was well, and there was no hanging, although in that day and place a travelling man could hang if but two or more should say he was from the road.

Now the lands of Lord Airlie were wide and far, of lonely pastures and paddocks past the woods, so lone that a travelling man could slip in his horses by night for a feed of grass, as easy as a man may do it now in a farm-field. But in those days it meant hanging, for anyone who came off the road.

Now, this night Tawny Charlie came to a lonely paddock far from the Airlie house. And he slipped in the horse he was riding, to graze all night beside a tall young colt the high lord Airlie kept there. And the next night the same. And the third night, on his way past the paddock, Charlie Graham laughed at the things in his own mind.

To steal the tall high-bred colt would be easy, for Charlie would need but to whistle, and ride the colt where he wished. But would all the countryside wonder who had taken that colt? Not they, no, because all would know the colt was gone with Tawny Charlie.

But this was the thing that Charlie laughed for. Because that third night, instead of stealing the colt, he gelded him, all quietly, and there was no noise or trouble, the paddock being far from the high house of Airlie.

Now weeks passed by, and the horse's wound was better, and all knew the high-priced colt was safe, because they could see him now and then, in the far-away paddock. Only it was not a colt any more, but a gelding. Its manhood was gone, and Tawny Charlie had gelded it, but the people could not see *that*, only that the high-bred horse was safe in the field.

It came on that one day the lord Airlie went laughing to Charlie in the horse-market of Perth, for Tawny Charlie to come and drink. Then Lord Airlie looked, and nearly fell, when he knew it was his own horse that Charlie Graham was selling before his eyes in Perth market.

So he spoke to the horse, and it answered him, and then he called the house-constable and two others, to seize Charlie Graham for selling his colt.

"Your colt, high brother?" said Tawny Charlie. "Will you mock me? *You* have a colt, and a good one, but I have none. Will you look at my horse, and say if he is yours, and if he be they can take me and hang me now."

So Lord Airlie looked, and laughed, and the liquor went

round for him and his friends and for Charlie Graham. Then after the drink Tawny Charlie sold his gelding, for a tree-top price, with the high lord and all his friends to praise it.

Then one day later the lord found his colt was stolen, but still never thought Charlie's gelding was the same. For how could it be?

Last night he had seen his colt in the paddock. To-day Tawny Charlie had sold a gelding in Perth Market, a gelding with no wound on him, a proper gelding of old time. Now, where was the other horse, the colt? Not stolen by Charlie Graham, for *he* was in Perth Market, selling a gelding, with Lord Airlie himself to prove it.

A mystery it was, and a great say. A mystery for long. Then the laugh came one night when there was drink, and Tawny Charlie told his cleverness. Because he knew he was safe.

The thing the lord loved best he would whistle away, be it woman or horse or tame black crow. Then the lord had laughed for the magic of the call, to praise Charlie that whistled even the bride from his bed. So Charlie knew he was safe, and told his cleverness.

Then they took him to Perth and they hung him. For a man may laugh if you steal his wife, but his horse—that's a different say.

CHAPTER FOUR

The Days of the Fays

SWAYING to the movement of a wagon-seat, rhythmic with each lift and thrust of the big dapple-grey's hams, lax to the stroking of the breeze and petted by the sun, I drowsed. There is no drowsing, no wakeful dream-feel, like the sleepy, lovely calm of a caravan-seat, in a warm afternoon on a lonely road.

Close by was the wall of Roman Hadrian, and the narrow road over it for Bewcastle Fells and the Border. At hand were the smooth leather reins, the edge of the wagon-door, and a scrap of curtain, fluttering friendly, came the road with me over the Roman Wall.

Before my eyes was the swaying back of the powerful dapple-grey, and alongside was the green screen of the white-thorn hedge, falling always behind and coming always along the road, like the window-curtain that flapped beside my face.

In front was the narrow road, where the grey kept the middle without guidance, and behind in the wagon John Fay and Lucretia were fighting, with words, but with crockery at hand.

It was their wagon, and the fight was no affair of mine, I

being a guest. Only I listened while I would rather have drowsed, because they kept me awake with their squabbling.

They fought because Fay was for taking the Bewcastle Fells, the high road for Scotland instead of the low. To call it the high road does not mean that the way is busy, for it is narrow and deserted, but only that it is more hilly than the other, the road by Riddings and Cannobie Lea.

No travel in the world equals the wagon-way. Already a stranger and alien to the place where you lighted your cigarette five minutes ago, but with the same horse-hams below you and the feel of the same smooth reins in your hand; homeless for ever, but with the smell of comfort in the same room always round you; for ever seeing a strange spire in the distance, and a new tree by the roadside, but with the same scrap of curtain fluttering beside your face—it is a friendly travelling.

Half dreaming always, hypnotized by the ever-oncoming surface of the road, it is easy to drowse, and still be awake to enjoyment, on a wagon-seat. Especially if others in the wagon be your friends, as Torry John Fay and his wife were mine.

Thus they could quarrel until sundown, for all I cared, about the high road and the low. I was there to talk with the Fays, and the Fays were with me whichever road we went. So I left the grey to plod the narrow lane, and left myself to listen sleepily, for what did it matter?

Then they finished squabbling, and Torry came to sit with me, to show me the road when we came to the fork. Because it had been agreed that they would take the high road to Scotland.

This Torry Fay got his nickname from his father and grandfather. Maybe from others before them, for all he could say. It might have meant that some earlier John Fay looked like a tower, and was called so. Torry was a solid and powerful man, and the nickname might have come in that way, since Torry is the Spanish gipsy word for tower.

Square and stiff-looking because of the muscles, with a hard black boxer's face, and with the quick, darting, alert eyes of a forest animal, Torry Fay looked as wagon-men have looked for centuries back—the fighter, the pugilist, the gipsy boxer, a type known everywhere to house-dwellers who visit the prize-ring or see pictures of champions.

With some bad luck, on the roads and elsewhere, I had good at times. Part of my good luck was that men like Torry Fay made friends with me. Torry himself considers that I have more knowledge than most. Which is praise from such a man.

That was how I came to be driving his dapple-grey by Hadrian's Wall, going on for the high road over Bewcastle Fells. Torry Fay has more knowledge than most himself. Although he cannot read.

He sat inside the wagon-door, and looked out at the distant hills, seen above the Wall, and backing the line of its rise with a bolder rise, of land suddenly rugged after the lowlands of the Esk. Then he waved to the Wall and turned to smile at me.

"Your people and mine, brother," he said slowly, "that wall was made for. To keep us away from the Emperor's little towns. Up *there*." He waved to the distant hills.

I lit cigarettes. There seemed nothing else to do. But Torry was waiting for my say, and I had to give it.

"When that wall was built, brother," I said at last, laughing, "the Phelans would be crowded in some corner, Holyhead way, thrown out by the Roman legions. And the Fays would be somewhere—it might be north of Palestine—stealing poor people's camels and robbing a drunken legionary now and then!"

Of course, I laughed all the time I spoke. But even then Torry's black face went blacker, and he held the edge of the wagon door.

"A lie," he said. But he laughed too.

"That wall," I told him, "was built by poor devils of British slaves, flogged on by the whips of the Roman legionaries, to keep out the Irish who were then called the Scots. Your people and mine knew neither side of it."

"A lie," said Torry again, still laughing, and then calm. "For my grandfather's father had a friend who was the King of Scotland, and in Galloway the Fays came and went to and from Ireland. It is said," he added carelessly, "that they could have been the Kings themselves, but they thought it better to be friends instead with the man who was King later on."

"There is no King in Scotland," I told him, "and there was none in your grandfather's time."

"Well, his father, then," insisted Torry. "Or it could have been a day earlier. But this King was the friend of the Fays, in Ireland and afterwards. There is a say about it," he went on, more loudly, as if to shout me down. "There is more than one say. Besides, he gave a say about it himself, this King. And gave my grandfather a paper." He turned to watch my eyes. "A paper," he repeated triumphantly. "From the King."

"Listen, brother," I put in. "Every man who has even a passport can boast—in a manner of speaking—that he has a paper from the King. Remember, it might be one like that, talked into bigness down the years, as the say was passed on from one to another."

"It is an important paper," said Torry Fay doggedly. "It gave the Fays power to do as they liked in Scotland, and to rule over their own people. One say tells that this King was a wagon-man himself," he went on in a casual tone. "But he was a King, anyway—you *must* know him, you that read printed books."

In Cardiff and Newcastle-on-Tyne, in Dundee and Glasgow and Durham, dozens of the Fays had told me the same story, and I knew the paper he meant well enough. But Torry was more of a student—a connoisseur of stories is the better description—than the others of his family. So I was glad to leave the grey to his own devices, and listen.

Torry's story was that the Fays were magicians, coming to Ireland from "down Greece way," crossing to Scotland in the days before the Roman Wall was built, driven north beyond the wall and back to Ireland, with a coming and going in and out of Galloway, between the many who fled to Ireland and the few who stayed by Bewcastle Fells.

All that part of it, in Irish mythology, is the story of the Milesians. In Ireland the tradition is that the Milesians came from Asia Minor, or probably Phœnicia. But every Fay in England and Scotland claims to have come from Ireland, and before that from the distant East. That part of the say Torry will have to fight out with the Irish historians.

The second part of Torry's tale is that some of "the Fays left behind" throve mightily in Scotland during the interval— an interval of centuries. That they never forgot they were travelling-men, and stood by their friends at need. Also that one of them, now a King, gave Torry's grandfather a paper to confirm all or most of Torry's story.

Somewhere in a caravan on the Border there may be, and almost certainly is, such a paper as Torry describes. In any case, it is unnecessary, since its existence is well known, and a corresponding document is in the records of the Scottish Court.

But it was given to one of the Fays by King James IV of Scotland, four hundred years before Torry Fay's grandfather was born. I said as much.

"I will give bad luck in a minute. Nant. In a minute," said Torry. "What is a grandfather or two? It was one of ours, a bit farther back—doesn't that make the say more true, brother? Doesn't it?" he pressed.

"It is over four hundred years ago," I objected. "The State records are there, and the paper is in them, since 1540."

"The paper is in a Fay wagon," contradicted Torry at once. "And not in anyone's record-house."

"The other part of the paper," I soothed him. "The part that proves your paper to be right."

"Good luck," commented Torry, and reached for the reins. "That say is settled then."

The fact that "his grandfather's paper" was really four hundred years older than he thought seemed to be the most natural thing in the world to him. For the rest of the way,

until the road forked for Cannobie and he was turning right
for the Fells, he talked about kings.

High treason would have been a mild description for the
things Torry had to say, if King James had been on the throne
of Scotland last week or last year as Torry assumed. This was
his say.

When the bulk of the Fays drifted back from Ireland they
found that the King of Scotland was 'one of their own.'
Wherefore the Fays were allowed to do almost as they liked.

Mildly I attempted to protest that Fay was not a Scots name.
Nor Irish, for that matter. Torry pointed to the sun.

"Am I to give you bad luck?" he threatened, and added the
word "Nant," which cancels the ill-wishing. "How many
names do men call the sun, even in Ireland alone, but he's
always there the same. Like the Fays. I tell you they were
magicians. Surely, brother," he coaxed, "surely a magician
can change a name, if he can change a tall dapple-grey horse
into a toad. Besides," he added darkly, "there would be changing of names in the bad days, wouldn't there?" I kept silent
and allowed him to proceed.

The son, or grandson, of the original king-friend forgot
himself, and "gave a say that all the wagon-people were to be
put off the road."

"It will be easy, brother," I laughed, "it will be easy for us
to agree about *that*. For was there ever an unfortunate king in
the world who hadn't to make a law like that, at some time or
other? It would be King James the Second of Scotland."

"Maybe," agreed Torry. "Him or another. He didn't live
long after," he appended, darkly again. Then he dropped into
the singsong tone used by all the wagon-dwellers when
repeating a conversation or quoting a record. "Not long he
lived, and the son was fair enough, and *his* son better still, that
gave the good paper to the Fays, saying they were kings and the
like, over the travelling people. Then the next son was better
than any of them, but for the one thing—he wanted to come
back and be a wagon-man again.

"Now, the Fays on the road, and the Fays in the tents, would have been pleased better far if he stayed in his palace, and gave out the gold money, and played with his golden crown. But not he. No. Out on the road with him, every chance he got, slipping away with the wagon-men or sleeping in the tents of the Fays. And him a king."

I waited. There had been nothing about this in any of the other Fay stories.

"Now, one night," pursued Torry, "the big drag of the Fays sat around their fires in the forest above Wemyss, in Scotland, far from the palace and far from the guards. With the King tall and tawny as the rest, sitting in the middle of them to eat and drink and laugh.

"But the houses will pull a man down, brother, even if he be a good black Fay to start with. Aye. Pull him down until he is no better than a house-louse. For what does the king-man do but reach his hand under Lucretia Fay's petticoat, Lucretia that was the mort of John Fay my grandfather.

"John Fay was for passing the king-man the bottle of Spanish wine at that moment, when the house-Fay that was a king forgot himself. So John Fay cracked the wine-bottle on the King's skull, and would have kicked his heart out but the family said no, that a king was a good person to have for a friend, and to let him go.

"But Lucretia gave her say, and told that if they did not mend the King's manners she would geld him herself with the black knife out of her hose. So they loaded the King with a pack on his back, and gave him a kick or two behind, and made him carry their pack right across the forest of Wemyss.

"Then next day they let him go, and said all was friendship again, but never to forget himself any more, by a travelling-man's fire, behaving like a house-louse or a ranting jack donkey.

"So the King was sorry, and gave his say to be all good friends again. That was his say, as a king and a man.

"The kind of man you will know, brother. *This* kind. With his soldiers he hung Garra Fay and John Fay at once when he got back to his palace.

"That night he gave a say and made a law. And this was the law: wherever in all Scotland three travelling-men were found together, then two were to be hung or shot at once and the third go free."

Torry Fay sat up on the wagon-seat with a start, as if he had been half asleep.

"Well, brother?" he demanded, in his ordinary powerful tone, and not in the singsong voice. "Well, brother, is that a new say to you, about the dirt that will come out from inside a man after living too long in the towns?"

"The story is known," I told him. "But no one can prove or disprove it. The law was made as you say."

"And worked?" pressed Torry. "It was worked, that law?"

I did not know, and said so.

"But if the law was used against any of your people," I pointed out, "and if they used their own names, the story will be there, in the State papers."

"Papers can be burnt," said Torry sullenly. "You cannot burn ten thousand men and women giving a say—although that one tried it and worse, that one who wanted to be a king and a travelling-man at the same time, and was only a ranting jack donkey."

I smiled a little, tolerantly, and made mildly protesting noises.

"He tried it," shouted Torry Fay, and drew the grey horse to a standstill at the fork of the road. "He tried it, brother. As did his black sons and their black sons. Bad luck."

He paused, and did not add the word "Nant," which makes the curse a jest.

"Tried it," he said again. "Hung the Fays, and flogged the Fays, and sold the Fays for slaves. Hung their sons and flogged their mothers and sold their daughters. Hung their grandsons and tortured their kin, down the years. All, brother, all because John Fay would not let the king travelling-man ran with his mort beside his own fire."

He panted, the hard black boxer's face set in a murderous mask, then breathed more easily, and smiled. With his long plaited gipsy-whip he waved to the right, to where the road climbed into the hills.

"Bewcastle Fells, brother," he announced. "Your road is west, for Cannobie." He gathered up the reins as I slid to the ground, and Lucretia looked out from the wagon window to smile good-bye. Torry made the parting-sign of the travelling people, open right hand by his shoulder, and turned the grey for the Bewcastle road.

I waited until the caravan was out of sight. Then I hurried, not on my road into Cannobie, but into Carlisle to seek a library, for books about the James kings of Scotland and the Fays of the Scottish roads. Two days later, questing older volumes, I was in London at the British Museum.

The books held a terrifying story, worked over and authenticated by the Rev. Andrew Small, Sir Walter Scott, David McLauren, Walter Simson, James Simson, and a host of others. There was no fundamental contradiction of Torry Fay's history.

Small's *Roman Antiquities of Fife* commented on James V's extraordinary liking for the gipsies. In one reference the King is censured for having actually knighted a wagon-man. There is an earlier record of the King having entered into a treaty with John Fay, or John Faw, directing "our said sheriffs, stewards, baillies, provosts, aldermen and bailies of boroughs" to assist John in his dealings with other members of the travelling clan.

Here with a vengeance was Torry's "paper" giving his ancestor powers to govern the wagon-people. But there was more.

The elder Simson tells that James V was nicknamed "The Gaberlunzieman"—or "Beggarman"—because of his habit of taking to the road and living with the travelling tinkers.

He narrates an incident when the King got into trouble with a tribe of tinkers near Wemyss, because of an indecent approach to one of the girls.

James V, or the Gaberlunzieman, was, according to Simson, compelled to carry a "grievously heavy pack" for most of a night, and was then dismissed "with scorn and contempt." The same author tells that James V immediately issued an Order in Council declaring that, if three gipsies were found together, one was immediately to be hanged or shot "by any of his Majesty's subjects that chose to put the order into execution."

Small, in his *Antiquities*, asserts that the law was that *two* should be hanged or shot, and one let go free. Furthermore, an act passed on June 6, 1541, against "John Faw etc" condemns the whole family, wherever found, to be banished from Scotland or put to death.

That was James V. He did not, as Torry put it, last long. In less than a year he was dead. For a time there was no king in Scotland, but a Regent, and the Fay family managed to have their "paper," the treaty between John Fay and James IV, recognized by the new Government.

Ten years later the Fays were still in good standing, and when thirteen of them were arraigned under James V's law they were all acquittted. The names of the thirteen are interesting to-day for anyone who knows that the roads of England and Scotland still carry the wagons of the Fays, the Colins, and the Browns.

The thirteen are Andro Faw, captain of the Egyptians; George Faw, Robert Faw and Anthony Faw, his sons; Johnne Faw, Andrew Nicoah, Sebastian Colyn, George Colyn, Julie Colyn, Johnne Colyn, James Haw, John Brown, and George Brown, all Egyptians.

Thereafter the Fay story is one of almost unrelieved gloom. James VI (James I of England) immediately he came to power issued edict after edict directed against the gipsies, imprisonment and death being mentioned as commonplaces, the most

merciful decree permitting the people—and their children—
to be employed at forced labour on public works. The leaders
of the gipsies came in for special severity. The Fay family were
the leaders.

There is a dreadful monotony about the records. On July
31, 1611, "four persons of the name of Faa" were sentenced
to be hanged. On July 24, 1616, two persons named Faa and
one named Baillie were condemned to die. In January 1622
Captain John Faa and five other men named Faa were sentenced to death. Some days later John Faa's widow, Helen
Faa, with Lucretia Faa and nine other women of the family,
was condemned to be drowned.

So the record goes on, from generation to generation. It is
easy to imagine them, those families of Fays, on the road in
Scotland, with the small boys and the girls learning the say as
they grew up, and knowing what they had to expect when
grown. Stray survivors here and there would pass the tradition
on, go themselves to the gallows, and leave children to grow
up, for the gallows in turn.

Always in the say, as with Torry, the emphasis would be
on the first chapter of the terrible story, where the hanging of
the Fays started from the spite of one mean man in power.
One mean man, punished for pawing his host's wife, reveng-
ing himself on generations of Fays.

Through it all some survived, and the Fays are still on the
road. The black fighting Fays—now I will remember the
dark face of Torry my friend, by the road-fork below Cannobie,
and know it is a good thing James the Fifth of Scotland has
been in his grave four hundred years.

The Fays have long memories, and tradition is indestruc-
tible. It is pleasant to know that the scholars will back the say
of the Fay who cannot read, pleasant to think that, although
the Gaberlunzieman is centuries dead, still a John Fay and a
Lucretia Fay go the road above the Border.

CHAPTER FIVE

The Price of Houses

THERE is a quiet part of Buckinghamshire, a big town-empty square, where I would like to make my home if I had a home. Not staying in one place, of course, because all the black things of life come from doing that, but moving about in this big square with the towns of Bicester, Towcester, Dunstable, and Aylesbury at its four corners, and with only the old town of Buckingham in the middle, all lonely.

Not staying in one place, but making a home in that region, if I should have a home, drifting over that north half of Buckinghamshire—that would be good. Only the tract must be three hundred square miles in size if it is an inch, and a man cannot have a home three hundred miles square. So he must have one three million miles square instead. Or stay in one place.

That last is not so good. Except for those who have new minds. Because in the old way—this is not a say whether it was a better way or worse—in the old way all the ugly things one man could wish another went into the condemnation that he must stay in one place.

When we punish, or doom, or torment another man we

rule that he is to be in one place only. In the towns things are changing nowadays. But until lately, when a town-dweller punished his enemy or victim or former friend he compelled the other to stand still.

Everything bad that one man could wish another used to be centred on that idea. Where would one put his enemy, his false friend, the man he feared, or the stranger who might harm?

Marooned on a rock. In a madhouse. In hell. In a cemetery. In a gaol. On a hospital bed.

Always when we want to hurt we compel the person hated or feared to remain motionless. Even when we are being cruel to a child we will force it to stand still, beyond nature. It is an old law of the jungle, older than men—look at a dog or cat dominating another, or think of our own first words to a dog who may bite: "Lie down."

So with our human enemies. Graveyard, prison, bedlam, or inferno—they are all places where the ultimate injury is done by keeping a person immobile.

But things are changing. People are becoming group-minded. For most it is now an uncomfortable business to be away from the crowds. We live and die in crowds, do our work in giant factories, go in tens of thousands to football-game or holiday camp, dwell for preference in vast blocks of flats, find our pleasure in numbers.

It is a strange modern perversion really, although it is leading to radical and probably beneficent changes in the human race. The old law of the jungle is being turned topsy-turvy, and from hurting others we now turn to hurting ourselves.

One of the most amusing aspects of the change is that we are in fact more and more preoccupied with doing harm to ourselves—as we used to do it to others—by insisting on confinement to one place. Even our stories and films tend more and more to have such themes.

A tale about a madhouse will be more popular than any

D

story of pleasant places. The graveyard is more desirable than ever before, for ourselves instead of our enemies, and the mounting suicide figures emphasize the desirability. Stories and films about prisons are hankered for. Manacles and the flogging-triangle are studied avidly—and not only by the ultra-neurotic who study the weapons and methods of those who hurt masochists for money.

It is civilization. Civilization growing up, and pressing forward to its logical conclusion. Of course, it is a good thing—for civilized people.

But for the wild people, the wagon-folk, it is a good thing too. Because the townsman no longer punishes the vagabond by making him stand still. He wants to stand still himself. So he punishes the wagon-man by casting him out from the crowd, compelling him to move ever onward. Thus every one is satisfied, and the present rule is good for all

In the old days, when honest cruelty and the lust of power over another's body and the will to wound were the law of life, there were bad times for those on the road. Especially when the towns were coming to be of unwieldy size, and were not over-comfortable.

The housemen kept in their towns, under compulsion. Growing puny and white-faced, forgetting the taste of food, forgetting the true feel or knowledge of physical love, terrified of the dark and terrified of insecurity, they kept in the towns. Naturally, they hated and envied and feared all those who were unlike them.

There were terrifying days for the travelling-people.

No country in the world has a clean sheet. The torture and maiming and murder of the vagabonds has been going on unchecked for centuries, ever since the first tiny village in the world was ringed round with its fence and the beginners, the pioneers of house-dwelling, crouched inside.

Safety was within the fence and the walls. Danger was outside, in the darkness and the wild. Listening, perhaps, to camel-bells at night, or hearing the stamp and snort of far-away horses, the first town-dwellers would build a fear-mythology centred always on the nomad, the vagabond, the out-dwellers.

From those puny beginnings came the first towns, to grow with a waxing and waning through the centuries into the mighty caravanserais of Bagdad and Babylon, Sidon and Tyre. The housemen were not cowering now—or not cowering all the time. But the nomads, the vagabonds, paid dearly for the housemen's fear of bygone days.

When the cities grew and spread westward, and there was no more fear that the nomads would sweep in one night to destroy and kill and burn and rape, the housemen still held the ancient fear. From the security of Rome and Paris, from safe-walled Warsaw and Leipzig and London, they gave the law and made the rules, still with the smothering fear of the out-dweller, the vagabond—almost non-existent then, but dreaded for all that, because the fear was older than those who felt it.

Masterless men, vagabonds everywhere, were hunted and tortured beyond belief, in Italy, in France, in England, in Germany—wherever the towns were growing big.

Some historians call it the natural process of civilization, but there is no need to be afraid of the facts, or to hide them behind nice words. It was the natural fear and hatred of an abandoned way of life, instinctive and inevitable as the antipathy between wolf and sheepdog.

It was fear—baseless, but all the more powerful for that.

In Britain the documented story of the fear, and of the cruelties in which that fear expressed itself, makes one of the most horrifying chapter in all history. The bulk of the hatred was directed against the so-called 'gipsy' families.

Few and unarmed, uncomprehending and powerless, roaming the roads, they were subjected to a persecution almost incredible. The acts and facts of that persecution bulk largely in any long say given by the old women, on the roads of England or any other civilized country.

Only in the civilized countries is the thing seen at its worst;

in a wild land the nomads will be on equal terms, or will have the upper hand. It is only among the big house-towns—where the vagabonds are few and impotent—that all the horrors of cruelty are loosed.

When the little girl of the Bakers lisped my name and gave me good luck it was no accident. Her infant mind would be fitting the story about Charles and myself into a pattern. In a hundred says about persecution and torment a few would stand out on the other side. Here was one, where the Irishman had let himself be 'plucked' to save hunted Charlie Baker.

Neither the child nor those who gave the say would know what the reader knows, that it was simply a case of my choosing the lesser of two evils. Among the other stories that one would stand up as a treasured exception.

What kind of a race-history must a people have, in which a trivial incident can assume epic proportions because it contradicts the general rule of hatred and persecution? Part of the answer is in the story of the Scampe leader. For his ancestor to be hanged, and later proved innocent, was a commonplace story, unusual only because some one in fact took the trouble to present the proof.

Millions of harmless or useful grass-snakes are kicked to pulp or hacked to bits, generation after generation, in Britain. Because our remote ancestors, in God knows what tropical land, were terrified of cobras and asps. I know no better parallel.

In Britain not long ago, and in accordance with a law never by name repealed, gipsies were to be put in irons "for as long as they have any goods of their own to live on!" In Scotland they were to have their ears nailed to a post, were then to be banished the country, and, if found thereafter, hanged.

All good citizens were ordered to "take, apprehend, imprison and execute to death" any person of gipsy blood. The only proof required by law was that "they are called, known, reputed and holden Egyptians."

That last law must have been a dreadful weapon in the hands of a blackmailing official. It was so fatally easy for a personal enemy—or even a pretty wagon-girl who spurned an official's advances—to be listed as a "known and reputed Egyptian."

There were even worse laws, notably a secret Order in Council issued by James VI. This commanded sheriffs to shorten even the pretence of trial, to "pronounce doom and sentence of death against the men." The men were to be hanged, the women drowned if they had no children. Those who had children were to be scourged through the streets and burnt on the cheek.

It was an orgy of cruelty, a national orgy, and some of the king's judges protested, asking for proof instead of hanging a prisoner on the mere hearsay that he was a gipsy. Those judges were rebuked, publicly and gravely, and immediately afterwards eleven people were sentenced to death "on the simple fame and character of being an Egyptian."

The laws of England and Scotland, from about 1609 until but recently, make dreadful reading for anyone who knows the road. Most dreadful of all for those who know the wagon-people well but are not of them.

It will be no secret to anyone who knows my work that I was at one time a tramp. Not a young man with a rucksack and a map, nor yet a well-feed author in search of Fleet Street, but a professional tramp, taking my sustenance from the road and moving at random. Thus I came to know the other classes of vagabonds. It is one reason why this chapter was written.

To a city person, naturally enough, there will be little difference between the professional tramp and the wagon-dwelling vagrant. That is, when the person is thinking of the Anti-Vagrancy laws, which through the centuries have been directed against the tramps and the gipsies alike.

There is in fact a vast difference—a fatal difference, as it has been for generations of gipsies. Of all the five classes who make up the road-population, the wagon-people have always been the most innocent and the most vulnerable.

The same five classes are on the road to-day, and every news-reader will recognize them when described. They used to be well known—superficially—at one time, and are described again and again, at great length, in the chief anti-vagabond laws on the Statute Book.

At any time for hundreds of years past a swoop on the road-populace would bring in five groups of people—criminals 'on the run'; lunatics and paupers escaped from institutions; work-less itinerants in search of employment; professional tramps; and wagon-people.

To-day the same thing holds good. Deserters from foreign armies, or from the British forces, are known to be on the road; now and then one is picked up for a crime of violence. Wandering mad people, or strayed paupers, are still numerous; the police collect them after a while, when starvation drives them into the villages. Men tramping in search of work are fewer; there is little unemployment at the time this book is written. The professional tramp, like the poor, is always with us. And wagon-people number about the same as they did in Elizabethan times.

Of these five classes, only the wagon-man has ever had any-thing to fear from the anti-vagabond laws. He serves as the scapegoat for all.

The criminals, needless to say, will not tramp the road openly. The lunatics and paupers do little harm except to themselves, and are picked up by the police after passing through two or three villages. The work-seekers look on the police and other officials as their friends.

As for the professional tramp—his papers are always in order. At any given moment he will be prepared to say, and prove, that he is the second mate of an oil-tanker, or an engraver on his way to a job, or an ex-sergeant-major about to call on his former commanding officer. (Or a journalist!)

In other words, whoever is going to be the vagrant and vagabond, the professional tramp will be able to prove that *he* is not. Nearly always the person described as a tramp is some unfortunate work-seeker who recoils in horror from the description.

Thus there is immunity, or coverage, for four of the five groups on the road. The wagon-dweller has no protection whatever.

There is his horse, and there is his caravan. He cannot slink into the woods like an Army deserter or a wanted man. Nor can he say he is looking for work and is on his way to the Labour Exchange. Above all, unlike the vagrant by trade, he cannot prove that he is a photographer or a ship's cook or a cinema organist.

Wherefore, since few village constables and perhaps fewer magistrates would understand the explanation given here, the wagon-people, through the centuries, have taken the blame for all vagabondage.

Damn it—they *look* like vagabonds, don't they, with their horses and caravans? Very well, then.

When the laws were directed against the gipsies as so described, when hanging was the penalty if some one merely *said* a man was a gipsy, or when the laws were directed against a single family by name, as in the case of the Fays, then the chapters of law-history are written in blood, the innocent blood of the Fays and Scampes and Colins.

Now the old woman's interjections about how easy it was to be hanged in the say of Tawny Charlie will come plain. Now the distrust and fear of the wagon-men for every house-dweller who looks like an official will be equally clear.

Unarmed, few in number, unlettered, industrious, and freedom-loving, they have been trained for generations, trained with only too good cause, to know that for some reason a city man was one who hanged your father, or gaoled your grandfather, or flogged your granny to death.

It is a black picture, but there is another side to it, all the brighter for the general blackness. Right down through British history there have been some families, wealthy and influential, who simply refused to obey or apply the murderous

laws they knew to be wrong. Small wonder that those names
have crept into the traditional lore, pathetically recorded for
ever, as a child will keep record of good and bad fairies, or
a robin make note of the house where there is no cat?

Stewart is a gipsy name, as it was the name of James the
Gaberlunzieman, who was a king. But Lovell—perhaps the
best-known 'gipsy' name of all—is nothing of the kind. It
is the name of a family who broke the laws, generations ago,
in defence of the travelling-people. The wagon-men changed
their name to that of their protector, and in the district formerly held by the Lovell family the Lovell wagon-people are
still spread far.

In the same way, Baker is really the name of a noble family
in Norfolk. For centuries the Bakers—that is, the landowning
Bakers—ignored the laws and showed friendship to the
road-folk. To-day the "Bakers of Norfolk" for every
travelling-man means the family of Charlie Baker and their
wagons.

Fay is straight gipsy, or even pre-gipsy. My own hazard is
that the Fays came from Thrace, that region where runaway
slaves and deserting legionaries and foundered camp-followers
from a hundred armies came in time to make 'a country.' But
where the Fays were before then no one knows, unless they
were part of the "mixed multitude" that went out from
Egypt with the Jews.

(Exodus xii, 38: "And a mixed multitude went up also
with them; and flocks, and herds, even very much cattle."
There were the Jews, the flocks and herds, *and* a mixed multitude. That last could have been the Fays.)

The Fays never changed their name, although for years
possession of that name meant a death-sentence. Mad pride,
as against the elasticity of the professional tramp or the swift
identity-switch of the other wagon people. Mad pride!

In some parts of England and Scotland that pride has been
respected. But mainly in districts where there are no large
towns, no cities, no shoal of officials to be proud with their

sheaves of printed forms that mean suffering to any out-dweller.

Such places are plenty in England, and one day the citizens elsewhere may be glad they are plenty. There is a big region of Northants, one that the tramps and tinkers and wagon-men call Hanslope Spire, after a church, although the place covers a hundred square miles. No town, except the sleepy old-world town of Hanslope, just within Buckinghamshire. Hamlets and villages in plenty, and prosperous farms, among which the tramps or the wagons can come and go in peace. Because the people of Hanslope Spire are different.

The next and nearest is the 'white spot' on the maps of which I wrote earlier, from Aylesbury to Towcester, and from Bicester to Dunstable. The edicts and orders and secret instructions lashed with cutting words, long ago, at the people of that region. Because they were backward and careless and uncivilized, did not flog and drown and hang as by law required.

They are still backward and careless, in the same way, and the names of the families are told by the camp-fires, in pride and pleasure and satisfaction, when the old women gave the say about ancestors rescued or befriended, children hidden from the lash, old women screened from the drowning, on from the days of Tudor Elizabeth to the terrible time of spreading industrialism, only last century.

A pleasant region, and a placid people. A region cut by a thousand narrow lanes and but one main road, where a farm-wife will draw a breath of pleasure at the sight of a gipsy caravan winding slowly down a hill to the hamlet. Where the tramp in the lane is at least a strange face, the face of one who knows clean roads.

Above all, and astounding to anyone who does not know about people, it is a region where lies and pretence and deception show little profit. Not in North Bucks will the didicai girl meet the reward she may reap on the road near a big city. Not on the Bicester road will the professional tramp find easy money, but will deal with people who know vagabonds.

The wagon-people drift, in North Buckinghamshire, knowing there is little to be gained by hurrying. The tramps drift, assured that in all the district there is no profit for them, but friendship and their sustenance for the road and no more.

It is a quiet place, where a man on foot or a girl from a wagon might tell stories for the love of it, give a say because the say was there. Knowing well that the say brought no reward, or that the reward would come without it.

Perhaps twenty centuries of shifts and trickery, of impersonation, of stratagems like those of a forest animal, are behind the wagon-folk, in their struggle to survive against the apparently insane hatred and cruelty of the house-dwellers. There is relief and pleasure in the hazel-hedges and blackthorn rows of Hanslope Spire, or the region round Buckingham, where the jungle artifice of survival is no longer necessary, and where a wagon can merely follow the road.

Perhaps more than twenty centuries of story-telling and fiction-trickery are concentrated in the mind of the tramp. Since the days when blind Homer told his lying tales for food, or the Prodigal Son pretended he had business in a far country, the tramps have been tricking the world into letting them go the road. Tricking the world because there is seldom any other way open, what of the town-laws.

For them, as for the wagon-men, the hazel hedges and the thatch hamlets along the narrow lanes north of Aylesbury and east of Bicester bring the smell of clean things with them, and the knowledge that the road reaches along three hundred square miles of friendliness.

Up there I should like to make my home, if I had a home. Drifting the three hundred square miles, and meeting the wagons, and hearing—or giving—a say.

CHAPTER SIX

Nameless Orgies

WHEN a rake of wagons goes on through a village, with a four-wheeled trolley here and there in the line, and perhaps a flat dray at the front or rear, the people in the houses seldom see many of the wagon-folk. Nearly always the comment is that there were very few gipsies for such a number of vehicles.

On the other hand, rural policemen and cottagers are aware that the people seen with the caravans on their journey are only a small part of the wagon-family. A skeleton staff as it were, mainly consisting of children and old people. The rest of the band will be scattered on the roads and lanes, often far afield.

Five caravans, two flat drays, a low trolley, and a troop of loose animals make up a convoy that straggles over perhaps half a mile of the road. The first casual thought is that it takes a vast number of wagon-wheels to carry a very few people. But when the family is glimpsed by its camp-ground at evening the observer goes to the other extreme, and wonders how on earth so many persons can be crowded into only five wagons.

Between townspeople and wagon-dwellers, living side by side throughout the country, there is the most complete cleavage. Literally and simply, neither party knows how the other lives. Any reader may test it, with some amusement.

At its camp-ground a family with the vehicles described just above will have by its fires a number of people astounding to a town-dweller. There will be an old man and his wife, the heads of the family, with perhaps two sons and two daughters, married and of middle age, each pair controlling their own wagon. For each of the four middle-generation pairs there will be an average of five children. The old couple's family is, of course, counted already, in the heads of the various wagons.

Between thirty-five and forty people will sit by the fires. The old man and woman, four middle-aged men with their wives, twelve adult men and girls, six children between eight and thirteen, and perhaps a dozen younger children, of every age from one to seven, may share the evening meal.

It is a heartening and even a thrilling sight for a city dweller to see the carts and caravans backed into a semi-circle, perhaps with the branches of a big tree spreading overhead, while the wood-smoke goes up through the leaves and the firelight flickers on the near-by hedges and trees. A second glance round the camp almost invariably brings the question—where, and how, and with whom do all the people sleep?

There are a hundred answers in the cities. Some of the conclusions and deductions will be familiar to news-readers everywhere, and to those who have heard wagon-life discussed among town-dwellers. That so many different explanations exist is sufficient comment on their exactitude.

Precisely similar ignorance and guesswork prevail among the majority of the wagon-folk with regard to the life and habits of people in towns. It is literally true that thousands of wagon-women, up to eighty years old, have never lived one night in a house, have no more idea how and where and with whom the house-people go to bed than the townsfolk have about the wagon families.

The theories and guesses on either side are vastly amusing,

fantastically incorrect as a rule, and—naturally, perhaps—uncharitable in the extreme. Prurience is a mild word for the speculations of a respectable middle-class housewife, and the speculations of a respectable good-grade wagon-woman, about each other's private lives.

There is nothing to choose between them. For years I have argued with a virtuous fortyish school-teacher of my acquaintance, endeavouring to prove that incest is not actually compulsory in caravans. Without avail. For years I have tried to convince Granny Marla Law, an ancient wagon-woman who is my friend, that the duties of a city girl, in office or factory, do not include the functions of a courtesan, daily and nightly and all the year round.

The debutante in Mayfair and the wagon-girl on the Great North Road are strangely alike. Especially when it is a case of imagining each other's intimate privacy.

My schoolteacher friend—naturally, I suppose—works it all out by mathematics. Here are five caravans, each with one bed, to hold perhaps four. Here are forty people, twelve of them small children, six of them in-between ages. That leaves twenty-two people, of whom five couples are married, the others grown-up men and girls. Five into—— And so on.

Granny Marla Law displays equal tolerance. A large modern factory in her view is not a place in which razor-blades or brushes or cigarettes are made. Or not merely such a place.

No geisha-girl in Japan, no houri of a Moslem paradise or dancing-girl in an Oriental harem, ever lived, or could possibly live, the life of a city-wench by day, according to my friend. Then at night—words fail.

There they are in the towns, by hundreds and thousands, by thousands of thousands, young girls with scent on their silk (!) clothes and paint on their mouths, young men who never walk even one mile of the road to be lean and lissom but keep in the houses to come sturdy. There they are, by thousands on thousands, enough to pack the road from York to Gloucester. And where do they all sleep?

My wagon-granny and my schoolteacher between them could furnish a dozen volumes of pornography, if either was anything but a reputable and virtuous woman. In vain I tried to advocate a little tolerance one day when four brown-faced girls and four tall, healthy young men passed, going the road. It was no use.

"Burnt brown—grown girls burnt brown by the sun, legs and all," said my friend censoriously. "Sunburnt all over, and shameless with it. Lusty young men—*young* men—always on the road with them.

"And look how those shameless girls go along the road, swaying their hips and tossing their heads to draw the young men's eyes. Flaunting their full, high bosoms, and with their brown legs naked halfway to the hip—going the road with men.

"There they go, four of the men, you see. Four. With the girls. Every one brown and lusty and laughing, stretching their shoulders and turning their eyes on the girls and laughing along the road.

"Along the road for days and weeks at a time, together— you can't tell me it's right. You can't tell me, just because you've lived among them, that all your precious sun-brown healthy people keep away from one another. On the road all day, and staying at the same places, together, each night. And what I want to know is—where do they all *sleep*?"

She went inside and slammed the door angrily, without waiting for an answer. But a second later she spoke from a window, to add a final thrust.

"Thousands of them on the road," she insisted. "All like those shameless pairs. But don't tell *me* how they all sleep— I know!"

The window-curtain dropped into place with a jerk, and there was silence. There was nothing to do or say. I looked up the road after the four brown girls who had gone on with the men. Then I sat down on the shaft of the caravan and waited for Granny Marla to recover her temper until I should try again to explain the innocence of the holiday hikers and of the National Cyclists' Union.

With my schoolteacher I encountered a similar outlook. Of course, there is much to be said on either side. But it is very funny, nevertheless.

Most of the caravan people are quite incapable of understanding how an office or factory *works*. No amount of argument will convince them that people will really go, without physical compulsion, to stand for hours beside a machine in a factory, or sit for hours making nothing in an office.

Such of the men as have been in prison (a fair percentage; it is still extremely easy for a wagon-man to get into gaol) know and understand what factory work in a prison is like. But they count it as an offshoot of the treadmill, about which they have heard in the various says. That the same thing should go on in freedom, without clubs or handcuffs for inducement, is to them incredible.

Any employer, any Labour Exchange official, will condense the discussion into a single terse phrase—gipsies are unreliable factory personnel!

The average bank-manager, turned out into the woods at midnight with a handful of snares, and instructed to find tomorrow's breakfast, would start on about equal terms with the wagon-man attempting to understand city life.

The caravan-women have less chance of ever grasping even the simplest facts about the functions of a modern factory. The clustering of thousands of well-dressed, lipsticked girls means at best a kind of perpetual Blackpool outing or holiday camp. Not once have I met a wagon-girl who understood that it was a way of life.

Scots highland people, and Irish peasants, have the same complete inability to understand industrialism. But *they* get over the difficulty in time—having several thousand years' start on the wagon-folk.

About home-life among the houses there is one basic misunderstanding which makes the wagon-woman thoroughly sceptical about the sex-morals of those who dwell beneath roofs. Few caravan-folk believe, or are capable of believing, that a house, however large, has more than one room to a floor.

With the evidence before their eyes of shops and cottages and taverns visited, they still fundamentally think of a house as one room, perhaps with one room above it in the big places. After all, a city housewife put to sleep in a caravan might— against the evidence of her own eyes—ask in the morning where the bathroom and lavatory were. It is the same thing!

Visualizing London as a vast congeries of those one-room places, with millions more people than rooms, the wagon-woman reaches the same level of understanding as the school-teacher, no more and no less.

Our own table-habits, toilet conventions, rules of dress, and bedroom customs are all deeply rooted, and have been worked out over centuries of practice. The sleeping-habits of wagon-dwellers are similarly fixed, are a matter of general and universal routine among the whole people. They are very simple, and, as one would expect, extremely practical.

Only once in civilization have I encountered anything resembling them. One night during the Second World War I got on a packed train at Aberdeen, bound for London. Eight of us, all strangers, sat in a compartment, facing the prospect of an all-night journey, sitting erect while a slow train covered five hundred miles.

There were two sailors, one soldier, myself, three Air Force girls, and a secretarial young woman from the A.T.S. We talked and laughed and told stories for the early part of the journey, until past midnight, and then, uncomfortably, uneasily, and with not the faintest hope of even a minute's respite, some of us began to sag in our seats. The soldier looked round the compartment.

"Wull onny o' ye be wantin' the licht left full on?" he inquired. "Or are ye a' wantin' to sleep?" No one wanted the

light left full on. The Scotsman looked round the compartment again.

"Sort yeersel's oot, then," he instructed. "Them that
doesna want sittin' to attention a' nicht." He turned to one
of the Air Force girls. "Come ower here," he ordered.
"And mind—no snorin'."

The other W.A.A.F. girls chose a sailor's arm and shoulder
each. The A.T.S. girl and I arranged ourselves in our corner.
The Scotsman lowered the light.

Presently the tiny compartment held four couples, clasped
in one another's arms, leaning close on each other's shoulders,
sleeping the dreary journey away instead of sitting stiffly in
torment. In half a lifetime of travelling I have never known a
similar case of adaptation among civilized people.

Of course, the wagon-people fare better than that. But the
whole economy of caravan life, developed through centuries
of selection, is directed towards a similar use of time and space,
of muscles and energies.

Ten young wrens can pack themselves in a nest the size of a
matchbox. As they learnt, so did the caravan-folk. That
Aberdeen soldier must have had wagon-wheels in his ancestry,
not too far back.

About the sorting out of the ages and sexes there is a similar
ease and practice, so deeply ingrained that it is no longer a
rule or convention but second nature. Age is not counted by
years or days, or by figures on paper, but by facts, as among
peasant people, fishermen, shepherd families, and others who
live near nature.

When a boy is the right age to go in the men's tent he goes.
When a girl is too old to stay with the children she goes in the
tent with the grown girls. Any organizer of a big school-camp
will known the same problems and the same solutions.

It would be easier, far easier, for a middle-class father to
mistake his daughter's bedroom than for a wagon-man or
wagon-girl to sleep in the wrong tent. Indeed, nothing will
convince my ancient granny-friend that middle-class daughters

E

and fathers and brothers do not in fact make such mistakes continually. Even while she takes the truly marvellous organization of the wagon-people for granted.

The accusations of mass immorality, of promiscuous animalism, so continually levelled against city people by the old women of the roads are profoundly amusing. Actually there is a little more sex-freedom in the cities than among the wagons, but of course the young townswoman enjoys no such licence as is generally supposed by those who live on the roads.

Still, the people who live over wagon-wheels can feel that there is something wrong in the city's complete break with natural existence. A female badger, or a doe-deer, simply *cannot* stray into casual mating. The cock pheasant knows where the hen pheasant is at any moment of the day or night, as the wagon-people know one another's whereabouts. But among the houses—at that point the old women's imaginations turn loose!

Immorality is as common among gipsies as among partridges or otters—that is, they have not yet discovered it. There are stringent marriage-laws, true, and censorious tongues wag industriously among the caravans as in suburbia. But the dice are heavily loaded against anything like sex-freedom, one saving factor being that girls marry at an early age, if they want to. Another is that, paradoxically enough, anything like complete privacy or seclusion is almost unknown in the wild.

Early marriage, physical health, and the absence of restraint result in an illegitimate birth-rate of practically nil. This among a people whose reactions to birth-control are the same as those of Roman Catholics. Knowing sex at first hand and thoroughly, in horses and people, the young wagon-women have few complications. In the majority of cases the girls are virgins until marriage.

I am opposed to this myself.

Also, I think the average city girl is physically a little happier. But then I have lived more than half of my life in the houses.

In such a general environment naturally there is no such thing as romance—that is, romance as known to us. It is literally true to say that a wagon-courtship takes place in one second, with one glance of the eyes. Many of our own stories and songs dealing with 'love at first sight,' as we call it, naming it for something unusual, come from gipsy songs and stories in which there are *no* love-speeches, no reiterated questions and protestations and promises.

Simply the wagon-girl knows love and lives it.

In the cities a vast amount of mating takes place in the same way. Then, afterwards, we remember, and hasten to use the set phrases. I seem to hear one of the Cannadine girls saying it does no harm, no harm at all!

With all our conventional *modus operandi* of the love-affair eliminated, it follows that all the good wagon-says about love differ sharply from our own. Instead of a girl being questioned and pressed and pleaded with, and finally yielding, so that the event becomes a story, the wagon-say takes all those stages in its first stride, and commences at the point where the average magazine-story leaves off! Thus the love-tale as such is absent from the wagon-lore, and instead we will often have a say about family rivalries.

Unless, of course, there is a case of two good men wanting the same girl. But that becomes a say about fighting, of which there are plenty.

The course of true love always runs smooth, in the old green roads and along the lanes. The most usual impediment, and the main material of the says, is the antagonism of the young people's families.

In other words, *Romeo and Juliet* is the pattern-story of the roads, not *Vanity Fair*.

There is a say about Maddalene Tuohy, and about young Tamaro Colin, who came to her father's wagon one night, outside Kendal and near Shap Fell.

The Tuohys and the Colins have been enemies since before the days of London, a long time ago. There is a say that it started in Ireland, before any Irish were there, when the Tuohy came from somewhere east and conquered that country—which was empty except for a Colin or two. There is a say that the Colins came one night and killed all the Tuohy, except two or three who grew up through a thousand years to be the strong Tuohy family of now.

Then there are a hundred other says, all about the two families getting the better of one another, up and down the years, on Epsom Downs and at the Fair of Ballinasloe, on Aintree Racecourse and over in Cushendall where you go to catch the Irish ponies.

That will be enough to show that the Colin wagons and the Tuohy wagons mix well on a camp-ground, like a bucketful of stoats thrown into a sack of weasels. And the say was given that never a Colin should draw free breath in a Tuohy camp as long as grass grew or water ran.

Now the Tuohy were camped one night below Shap Fell, and the Colin wagons were thirty-odd miles away, over the mountains and past the lakes, on the common beside Keswick by Derwentwater. So it would be quiet that night, anyway.

But Tamaro Colin came riding a horse from over Tebay side, making for Keswick across the fells. He rode by night, and kept to the bridle-tracks, on account of a small matter with the police at Ambleside. So he came down from Shap, pushing the horse hard, and what does he see pulled in at a lane-end but the wagons of the Tuohy.

Now, Tamaro was only twenty, but a big, powerful, good-looking boy, and cunning on the road or in the woods like all the Colins. Laughing and good-humoured most of the time, but there below the fell, by midnight it would be, he pulled the horse suddenly, and kept stock still, and snarled like a dog-fox cornered in a drain.

That was all natural, and right, for the Tuohy stole his grandfather's pedigree grey after the fair of Nenagh, in Tipperary, and kicked his uncle Garra nearly to bits at Epsom the year Orby won the Derby. So it was natural and right for the snarl to come on young Tamaro's mouth that night at the foot of Shap Fell.

Now, he was a mischievous young villain, this Tamaro Colin, one that would rather beat a man in the boxing-ring by a trick instead of knocking him cold. A trickster, and a laughing, good-humoured, handsome boy—if the snarl was off his face.

So he tied the horse to a stone by the side of the road and crept down to see would the Tuohy dogs come for him, or would they leave him talk. For all the Colin men can do things with dogs.

Now his luck was in, for the first dog that came was a young one. It came silently, and in one minute that dog and Tamaro were big friends. Then the Colin boy went softly a few yards and waited for the next dog to come. So one by one he got the Tuohy dogs round him, and they liking the smell of himself and the horse and the Colin dogs, and there was never a bark or growl as Tamaro crept up to the wagons.

He was a wicked young villain, and a mischievous laughing trickster at the same time, and when those two things come together, adding up to a snarl, some one is going to be sorry. To steal one horse and cut the throats of the rest would have been his delight, but the horses were somewhere out on the Fell. So he fixed that he would set fire to one wagon and drop the frightened Tuohy one by one as they came rushing out, and then the Tuohy would know whether a Colin could draw breath in their camp or not.

Gathering bundles of rags and weeds to put under the caravan, he sneaked about in the camp like the shadow of an ash-tree, when some one moved to come outside from one of the tents. Tamaro froze in a patch of shadow, with his holly-cudgel ready and the snarl on his laughing face, to wait.

It was a tall girl, and she walked a few yards from the tent to the side of a stream, and Tamaro Colin grinned more wickedly than ever, changing his plan.

If he could get her before she screamed it would be easy to carry her up the fell, and this would be better than burning a wagon or cutting a horse's throat. He waited, while she looked round as if she wondered why the dogs did not come to her. Then she started back to the tent.

He had her, with his big left hand over her mouth, before she could utter one squeal, and started to drag her away. Like a wildcat she fought him, and her wearing nothing but shoes, so that he could hardly keep hold of her. But young Tamaro was a powerful boy, and she could do nothing, so he got her away to the side of the road, where his horse was.

It was the toss of a farthing coin whether he choked her then and there, because he dared not take his hand from her mouth, and that way it was hard to put her over the horse. But he managed at last, and mounted still holding her, and away up the bridle-path to the lonely top of Shap Fell, with the laugh and the snarl coming together on his face, and all the black villain wickedness and cunning of him behind both.

There was nothing of softness in what he meant to do, but a black laugh for when she went back to the Tuohy in the morning. With all the wagon-people in England to laugh at the story, and watch her growing for nine months, and then the Tuohy would have a Colin drawing breath in their camp and be laugh-matter for ever in the says and at the gatherings.

So on the top of the fell, miles from the camp, he pulled the horse to a stop and got himself down. With one hand still on the girl's mouth, and one thumb on her windpipe, he spoke for the first time.

"You are coming down from the horse," he told her. "I will take my hand from your mouth, my Tuohy girl. But the other hand will stay where it is. So if you want to scream, scream, and everything else will be over before you're cold."

It was a wicked thing to say. But he was a wicked young devil. He let go her mouth, and she did not scream, but came down from the horse and stood before him in the moonlight.

It was not much of a moon, but enough for them to see each

other, him holding her at arm's length by the throat. They looked at one another, for a second maybe, and Tamaro let go her neck. It was one second, and there was not much of a moon to see each other's eyes, but there was love in that second instead of hatred.

"Your name, tawny one?" said Tamaro.

"Tuohy," she said, and added nothing. The snarl was back on Tamaro's face for a second, and then he laughed mischief again.

"From here to Vienna I suppose anyone would know that much," he grinned, "after one look at the wicked black face of your clan. Which Tuohy?"

"Maddalene," she told him. "And you are Tamaro of the Colins, the trickster."

"Well, tawny one," said Tamaro, without more ado. "There is the horse. Five miles back to your own wagons, and twenty-five to mine, at Keswick by Derwent. Come and be my mort, and we will ride to the Derwent together. Or say no and we will ride the horse back near to Shap, where you can walk the rest of the way. And then if you——"

"Give me the long coat off you, you fool," cut in the girl. "Am I to stand naked all night on the fell, while you give an old woman's say about this road and that? Give me the long coat, and get up on the horse."

So he put the long coat on her, and they rode into the Derwent country before morning, and in among the Colin wagons about two miles out of the town. Now there was such a bustle and buzz in that camp, when they heard that Tamaro had caught one of the Tuohy, that you'd think every tent on the pitch had been over an ant-nest.

The old women were the kindest, being only for flogging the Tuohy girl with nettles and sending her into Keswick naked. The younger women thought of harder things, on account of this Maddalene Tuohy being a beauty, and riding thirty miles naked over the fells with their kinsman.

But the four hard black brothers of Tamaro laughed

wickedest of all, when they heard what Tamaro had intended to do, before he wanted Maddalene for his mort. Simon Colin, that had fought in every fair from Galway to Galloway, laughed merriest of all, and clapped Tamaro on the shoulder.

"That was a good say of yours, brother," he grinned. "That first say. And now there are five of us it will be all the better story for her to take back to the proud flaunting Tuohy. A good say, brother."

"There will be coffins in that say," put in Tamaro quietly, and reached for his shotgun. "There will be four coffins in it."

So the brothers laughed when they knew the woman was to be Tamaro's mort, and there was no more to be said. Only Vingie Colin, the slant-eyed girl that had thought she would be Tamaro's mort herself, would have none of their softness.

Vingie was a wicked one, with a spiteful tongue and a hard, small cunning to wound. Sour inside her she was, because of an eye-slant and a chest-flatness that made her hate the other girls of the wagons. So she hated Maddalene more, and she remembered every say that bade the Colins hate the Tuohy. Every one, back to a deadly club-fight in Ballinasloe, two hundred years back, and she was for cutting off Maddalene's breasts at least, and then to let her go back to her own people.

But while the Colin-kye were talking there was a rush and a clattering, with the women crowding into the caravans and the men grabbing for clubs or iron bars or stakes to defend themselves. Because twelve of the Tuohy, on horses, had come over the fells hotfoot and swept murder-mad into the camp.

With a catapult Simon Colin picked one off, twenty yards before he got in, but the rest came on with a rush, clubs and knives and two shotguns among them, and it was being a bad fight for the Colin-kye.

Five of them, young and old, were down and bleeding, with the Tuohy coming on in a line again, roaring mad, Luke Tuohy at the head, Maddalene's father, and big Sim

Tuohy, her brother, beside him. Townspeople hid, and the few town police kept the edge of the camp, able to do nothing while the Tuohy swept down to finish the fight.

Swinging the holly-cudgel for Tamaro's head, Luke Tuohy snarled black vengeance to end the hated one. Then two shots came from a caravan window, and Luke went down bad-wounded, and Sim dropped peppered with shot about the face, roaring in fury, and the fight was stopped with the police in charge, one grabbing the biggest young Tuohy and one grabbing Vingie Colin that came running from a caravan door with the shotgun in her hand.

So all ended peacefully in little time. For the housemen's police there was work that day, and the next day, with nine of the Tuohy and six of the Colins to be locked up for the fight, and with Vingie locked up the closest, for shooting Luke Tuohy and his son nearly to kill them.

The housemen's law is a strange one. For, by the housemen's law, no matter which Colin hit a Tuohy he was innocent, because the Tuohy were what housemen call the aggressors. A strange law, but fair in its own way.

So the Colins went free. All except Vingie. For the housemen's law is that you may hit an aggressor with a bottle if he come to aggress *you* with a bottle, but you must not stab his eyes with a skewer, or knife him, or shoot him. So Vingie they put in the gaol-house for a year.

Then soon there was laughing by the Colin wagons, for days and weeks, when Maddalene was Tamaro's mort. Happy he was, the black laughing villain, and happier she, the dark beauty of the Tuohy. Till they laughed together one day weeks later above on Shap Fell, but with the Tuohy wagons away for Surrey, when the two of them came by the place where Tamaro took his girl off the horse.

"A good place to remember, for a say, my tawny one," was Tamaro's word. "The fine days that started from here that night, and the fine good fighting by Keswick with your people and mine, to see who would have you."

They lay on the heather, and loved for a while, until Tamaro thought of the rest of the say.

"Poor slant-eyed Vingie," he said, and was slow to speak. "Poor vinegar-tongue, that saved us with those two shots, even though she hated your heartbeat, my tawny love." He looked up in half-anger, for Maddalene was laughing at him.

"Vingie," she said at last. "To shoot my father, and to shoot my brother Sim, and save the Colin-kye, and leave me to mate with the wicked, black, laughing, villainous trickster I love—aye, your kinswoman Vingie would do it, yes?"

She laughed again, and watched Tamaro's eyes.

"Maybe the tricksters know one another after all," she told him, and reached to stroke the black curls. "Poor vinegar Vingie was hot in haste that day, in haste to grab the gun—after I'd shot Sim and my father."

CHAPTER SEVEN

Luck and Logic

THERE will be no need to tell anyone that the wagon-people are superstitious. Living on moors or mountains, travelling in forest tracks or lonely lanes, knowing darkness and the things of darkness, it is easy for a man to shape his thoughts differently from one whose life is passed among lights and in the security of a house.

Riding on a small flat dray with Marly Coaper, along a high-banked Cornish lane, I learnt about superstition. The Coapers are the oldest of the Cornish tent-people, as the Cornish tent-people are the oldest and hardiest of all the wild-dwellers in Britain. The difference between Cooper and Coaper is the same as the difference between Price and Rice—the second name is the ancient original.

Marly was fifty years old, a hard black man who did not often smile. He was angry with me, as our pony trotted along the lane near Menheniot, on our way back to the Coaper wagons. Also—which was much worse—he was rightly angry. I had said 'God bless' to a gipsy at the end of a small monetary deal.

People in almost every walk of life use that phrase, in Britain and Ireland and the United States. Broadcaster, stockbroker, news-editor, film producer, publican and postman and country bus-conductor—all use the words automatically, and with rather a pleasant effect of beneficent familiarity.

The late John Hilton, perhaps the most intimate broadcaster produced in Britain, always finished his talk with those two words. Some of the most sophisticated traders in the whole world, the car-salesmen of London and New York, often use the same phrase as a farewell, and it is a commonplace among journalists and actors.

Now I had used the words by a gipsy-man's fire in Cornwall at the end of a transaction. Wherefore Marly Coaper sat beside me on the dray in the lane, black-looking and silent. I should have known better. I *did* know better. So I was in disgrace.

The tiny, twisting, high-banked roads of Cornwall are strangely like the people who made them. Or perhaps not strangely.

For miles a narrow lane will wind and curve across the countryside, always between high banks which are as tall as a man. Green and lovely, loaded with primroses in spring and with violets later, the banks will almost intoxicate a stranger with the nearness of their beauty, so that he forgets his view is restricted to a few feet, that he can see little or nothing of the land around, only the spangled loveliness of the bank close by for mile after mile.

Then, if the soil be scratched, below the primrose roots it is found that the bank is really a wall of rock. League upon league of high-piled granite, walling in the lanes, goes snakily across Cornwall.

Lovely within limits, cut-off and lonely, granite-hard under the skin, the high-bank lanes and the Cornish people have much in common. The Coapers, strangers and nomads as they are, number themselves among the oldest of those who live in the primrose lanes of Cornwall.

Marly and I had been over to Minions, on the edge of Bodmin Moor, to dicker for a horse I wanted from one of the

Coopers from Trethevy. This Trethevy is an ancient place, with tombs and stones and monuments that were old when Julius Cæsar was born. Scattered about among the fields they are now, with cattle scratching against them or moor-ponies using them as shelter from the wind.

The structure called Trethevy Stone itself may well be one of the first *houses* ever made in Britain. The Coopers say it is.

Trethevy is simply a small place that might be a garage or henhouse nowadays, made of a few giant slabs of stone placed edgewise in a square, with another vast, flat stone laid on top of them for a roof. The peasant in whose field it stands would hardly use it for a stable. But at one time it must have ranked as a wonder, almost a miracle—the Canterbury Cathedral of an earlier age.

The Coopers, and especially the Coapers, will tell that it comes from the time when men first left the road, the days of the early building. Starting with Trethevy, men looked ahead to the time when they would build one house, stretching over all Cornwall and all Britain. They left the road, and escaped from the darkness, and abandoned luck.

It is one more case of a say that has been telescoped, centuries or millennia being omitted as the story is passed on. Building did not start in Britain, or even in Cornwall, which is a different thing, but came from the East, leaving Babylon and Cairo and Athens and Paris behind as it came westward. But the Coopers of Cornwall care nothing for that. Trethevy is one of the first houses, one mark of the days when men abandoned luck, and thought the darkness could not see them because they had a light inside Trethevy.

Every say wishing that God will bless another person or curse another person dates from those days, as the Coopers see the world. It is a complete break, an utter cleavage with natural things, destroying and defying luck, and setting in its place a careless phrase indicating that some god is to bless the hearer.

Thus complete is the division. Now by the fire of a man to

whom Marly Coaper had introduced me as worthy I had said at parting "God bless."

To cut his horse's throat would have been a smaller injury.

The dicker for the horse had been 'cooked' between Marly and myself in the pub at Menheniot before we went over to Minions. Even though I was a houseman (of sorts) I was not such a fool as to attempt the purchase of a horse from Garra Dunnaha, the white-haired, black-faced, shrewd old leader of the Coopers.

The name Cooper does not indicate the trade of barrel-making or tub-manufacture, but is really Coper or Coaper, meaning one who furbishes or fakes. Horses, generally. The first name Garry or Garra in fact means horse. So that a man called Garra Cooper—certainly I was not sufficient of a towns-man to try getting the better of *him*, with his horses round him on a lonely moor in Cornwall.

(It would be interesting to know if Mr Gary Cooper the film actor has wagon-wheels in his ancestry. Because if the name is his own and not a pseudonym every gipsy in the world will be taking him as a descendant of horse-copers.)

Marly and I had gone on to Minions with a plan cut and dried. Marly was to make the dicker, and get five pounds for himself if he concluded a profitable deal. Garra was not to know, but would certainly guess, just what had been arranged.

On the other hand, I was not to know, but guessed well enough, that Marly and Garra, talking with their eyes and hand-grips, would be dividing my fiver between them. Three pounds of it might stay with Marly, but two would certainly go to Garra—and two other pounds, to make up what Garra had had, would go on to the price.

It was all rather intricate. But I am a fair chess-player, which helped. And we had plenty of time, which helped more. At the end the deal was made to every one's satisfaction.

Then, like a fool, when we were leaving I said "God bless." There was silence by Garra's wagon as we came away.

Marly Coaper plainly wanted to be rid of me, as we went

down between the primrose banks into Menheniot. Fortunately, I can tell how I felt, so that readers in Britain at any rate will understand. The comic artist H. M. Bateman fixed the picture for years to come, with his drawing of "The Guardsman who dropped it."

Soldiers are being inspected on a glittering parade, where not a hair or thread, let alone a button, is out of place. One can feel that the soldiers are hardly daring to breathe, as the General approaches to review them.

Then one Guardsman drops his rifle.

That was how I felt at Menheniot. The man who said "God bless" to a gipsy horse-trader.

Luckily, I had a small dicker of my own to make with Marly, about the five pounds and other things, so I went to his fire instead of turning away in the lanes for Liskeard. After a can of tea and a smoke there was better humour, and I was able to explain that I meant no harm—that I had merely been a thoughtless fool.

Wagon-people are superstitious. Townsfolk are not. There is a whole world of difference in outlook.

Out on the roads, or in the darkness of a forest at midnight, any man may come to know, or at any rate to believe, that there are forces in the universe which can make or break him, if properly handled or foolishly defied. The road-guide and signpost called luck is of the first importance.

Luck is the waysign which decides whether the traveller's track will bring him to grass and water, or will lead instead under a falling tree or across a ford at flood. In towns men do not believe in luck. Which is natural enough.

The lives of men in cities are lived in accordance with reason, science, philosophy, and law. City men have precise knowledge instead of blind chance to rule their lives. Out in the darkness of the woods there is only luck for a guide.

True, the city people of Britain and America spend roughly a thousand million pounds each year on raffles and draws and sweeps, on astrology and fortune-telling and greyhound races, on horse-gambling and theosophy and football pools. At the the same time, it is a fact that city people do try to disown their superstitions, endeavour to rule their lives by science and law, and do not believe, or try not to believe, in luck.

The wagon-people, more simply, are superstitious. They believe in luck, all the time.

Thus one must never say "Good morning" to a wagon-man. If it is near noon, then the wagon-man has had his morning, good or bad, and to hell with your empty wishes. If it is past noon, then which morning do you mean, if you mean anything?

But to say "Good luck" to a person starting out on the road —that is a different matter. Even if you are a townsman, who could not be expected to realize the importance of the words. Much more if you are of the road, and know what you are saying. Now the full enormity of my offence by the fire at Minions will be plain. I knew.

Somewhere earlier I have said that the Reformation missed the caravan-people, although there were plenty of them in Britain and Germany when the Reformation occurred. Great as was that break between thought-ways, it had no meaning for the people on wagon-wheels, because they had known a wider and more complete cleavage, a greater reformation, long earlier. In the days when men first went inside Trethevy, choosing law instead of luck, science instead of superstition, houses and light instead of darkness and the road.

Now, it should be understood at once that the road-folk take us, who live in cities, for a collection of clumsy liars and foolish would-be swindlers! We are dangerous, true, because we can pass a law having gipsies hanged or flogged or gaoled. Only the danger does not come from our wickedness but from our folly. We are not to be trusted in anything, however small.

Not very flattering! But there is a lot to be said on the wagon-man's side. A thousand says, recounting a thousand dreadful items of history, help to confirm him in his views.

We of the towns have in fact behaved inconsistently for centuries.

The trouble is that our alleged abandonment of luck for logic and of superstition for science is such an obvious and flimsy falsehood. Our preference for house-life instead of road-life is equally shaky. Wherefore the gipsyman decides that we do not ourselves know what we believe or what we want, and he is afraid to trust us in anything.

What wonder, then, that the smallest gipsy child, coming to wheedle a sixpence, will automatically lie and pretend, if dealing with a house-dweller. What else is the child to do?

There is no word for 'truth' in the romani language. There is the crux of the matter. Truth is what we tell in the cities, when we say we are rational instead of superstitious, when we say we do not believe in luck, even while we buy an astrology-paper or post our football coupons.

But it is not surprising that so many of the wagon-wheel says and songs are about luck.

Things like these occupied my mind when I parted with Marly Coaper at his fire near Menheniot, and started up the narrow lane towards Pengover Green and the main road. Because, of course, I was going back to Minions, to make my peace with Garra Dunnaha.

A baker's van took me by Pengover and Penhawgyr across to within sight of Caradon Hill, and I walked across Caradon on the pony-track, which cuts nearly two miles off the road. Caradon is only a little mountain, about 1500 feet high, with wide heathery moors over most of its surface. But it carries the marks of no fewer than five ways of life.

Ponies roam on the moor, wild or half wild, as they were thousands of years ago. Gaunt, stark rocks, carved by some forgotten race, stand up here and there among the gorse. Trethevy Stone shows on a neighbouring hill, the cathedral of the stone-men, and a curiously obscene-looking rock, carved to resemble an intimate part of some giant's body, stands in the heather by the roadside.

F

To right and left, as well as on the top of Caradon itself, ivy-grown walls and tall grey turrets resemble the ruins of some medieval castle, but are really the shells of abandoned tin-mines. Tall towers, ivy-grown also, are the crude chimney-stacks of an earlier day. Broken railway bridges are by each road-crossing, and the moor-ponies gallop on a curving levelled path—the site of a vanished railroad.

The peasant farms are dotted in every valley where the encroachments of the moor can be defied, wherever grass may be grown instead of heather. While still another way of life grinds and shrieks of its existence on the top of Caradon, where a later generation of men have abandoned the tin-quest and are tearing out the stone entrails of the mountain, to be crushed into cement or road material.

Beside and below them, past the hamlets and the tillage, on the edge of the moor, older than all the other ways of life and still unchanged, the camp-fire of the Coopers smoked beside three black tents and two wagons. It was a good sight from up there on Caradon-top.

Neglected and perishing farms, the nameless monuments of the forgotten race who built Trethevy, the gaunt ruins of the tin-mines, the shrieking stone-crusher on the hilltop—they had all passed or were passing. But the tents of the road-folk were still on the edge of the moor. I hurried down into Minions and over the road.

Garra Dunnaha was not glad to see me, and showed it. But —some families have a way with horses, and some with dogs. The Phelans have a way with men and women. Also, I knew I had done wrong, and was anxious to put myself back where I belonged. In a quarter of an hour my peace was made and I was gossiping by the fire.

Fortunately, or sensibly, I chose to tell them two stories I knew about luck. They were already aware that I had come all the way back from Menheniot to explain my blunder, and that went far to reinstate me. But my stories were about a branch of luck known more to Irish road-people than to others, and, as all new says about fortune or misfortune are treasured, the tales completed my reinstatement.

There were nine people by the fire. Old Garra Dunnaha and his wife Phrania sat beside me, smoking continually, while their son Luby and his wife Marla watched me intently across the fire, missing no word or glance.

Mark, about twenty-one, and Jidbell, about twenty, the eldest children of Marla, laughed as I told how Marly Coaper had scowled at me on the way to Menheniot. Marly was their uncle, being Marla's brother. Sim and Larry, about fifteen, grinned sympathetic understanding, and Lonia, a small girl of perhaps twelve, kept her distance—waiting to see whether I brought luck or not.

I told them about gaysa, the special Irish brand of luck, the prize and monopoly of a few ancient Irish families. The Coopers of Minions Moor liked that idea. They are an old family and proud themselves.

Centuries ago in Ireland, before there was any Saint Patrick or Christianity, any houses or laws in books, the acts and facts of gaysa—or gesa, as it is spelt in the Irish way—were well known. There are many traditions, handed on from generation to generation, and there are also written records, of stories which, in the beginning at any rate, were told as facts and accepted as law.

One is the story of why the people of Araby never take salt in their porridge. My mother used to tell it, in, I suppose, the same words used by *her* mother, many of them out of place nowadays.

Gesa, simply explained, is a kind of bargain with Fate, a pact with the forces of the universe, a giving of oneself as hostage to fortune. Centuries later than gesa, the tradition about a man selling his soul to the Devil had the same basis. *Faust* is a kind of very thin gesa story—a houseman's version, as it were.

Naturally no house-dweller, believing himself free from superstition, could or would accept for an instant any of the beliefs implicit in the gesa-tales. Very seriously, I have a suggestion to make. Let any houseman go out at midnight into a wood he does not know, any wood, and walk through it for an hour. He will learn about gesa from the people and animals among the trees.

The Coopers by Minions Moor listened, and had no reservations about logic.

My mother's story is the Irish version of a tale well known to readers of the Old Testament. In the Irish tale a man and his wife had run away from the tents of their people, who were great magicians, to live in the security and comfort of a house. In Araby.

Then one night they were sitting in their comfortable stone hut, thinking how lonely and cold it would be out on the road, with no civilized comforts like salt for their porridge and a roof for their heads, when there was a knock at the door. A stranger stood outside in the dark, a man with shining feet that gleamed and glowed in the darkness.

He ordered them out, for the town was to be destroyed by the feys. They were to follow the gleam of his feet, back to the tents of their people. And he put gesa on them to take nothing whatever from the town, or they would die.

So the man and his family walked out as they stood. But the wife went unwillingly, reluctant to leave all the comforts of house-life. Thinking how dreary it would be to start off on the road next morning, with tasteless meal and brackish water, she fixed her mind on saving *something* to help on the road. So she grabbed a handful of salt on the way out, knowing the shiny-footed man could not see, and pleased because back on the road they would have salt for their porridge anyway.

Then on the fringe of the desert, when they were all safe, she got her dearest wish and was turned into a lump of salt herself. And from that day to this no one in Araby takes salt in his porridge.

Two of the youngest Coopers chimed in at once, having

heard the story of Lot's wife. While Marla their mother and old Phrania their grandmother smiled approval, they told the story as they had heard it in the Sunday-school at Tremar village. The Coopers liked the tale of Lot's wife, but the general consensus of opinion was in favour of my mother.

Of course, the dice were heavily loaded. My mother's family name was Colin.

The other gesa-story was personal, one that has been told in print more than once, by me and by other people. It was of an occasion when, naming cards drawn by himself, I caused a warder in a prison cell (and a condemned cell at that) to bow down like a heathen worshipping an image.

In town-language, it is the story of a marvellous series of flukes. In a cell where I waited to be hanged I was showing tricks with cards to a young warder. Partly by simple deduction and mathematical practice, partly by trickery because I had stacked the pack first, I named a whole series of cards chosen by the warder. He got angry, took the pack and shuffled it thoroughly, selected a card behind his back, and defied me to name *that* one.

Of course, the terms of the test were ridiculous, but they showed the state of his mind!

I named the card. Sweating in perturbation, he shuffled and cut again. I named the card again. Then he put his open hands before his eyes and bowed like an Indian child before an idol.

Flukes, of course.

Those last three words are written on a typewriter, in the comfort of a well-furnished room, with a blazing fire beside me and a good bright light overhead. Flukes, of course.

A hundred yards from where I write is the black outline of Assington Thickets, a clump of woods in Suffolk, almost impassable even by day, a real Sleeping Beauty wood by night, where the careless wayfarer might stand for hours among the closing brushwood, unable to move forward or back, almost

feeling the thicket growing closer around him as he stands.
I am not certain whether I should write the same three words
over there, although it is only a hundred yards away.

What the Coopers knew was that, if the cards had *not* been
the right ones, then I should have died then and there. Really,
it often happens even in towns, although we have nicely
sounding inquest-phrases for it.

A man puts gesa on something, or on himself to do something. If he fails and does not keep his gesa he dies, or if he
has reached out for too much and succeeds, then he keeps his
gesa and dies just the same.

We have an inquest-formula for the man who wins a
hundred thousand pounds in a lottery and drops dead. Or for
the woman who gains fifty thousand pounds in a football-
pool (she not believing in luck) and drops dead. Heart-failure
from excitement, the verdicts say, and it is a good enough
phrase.

Thoughtless gesa, the old women class it in Ireland. Calling
for too much good luck, the gipsies name it. It is the same
thing. Perhaps the inquest-phrase is the same thing, too.

The Coopers gave me my supper by their fire that evening,
and I went with Mark and Jidbell to look at "The Stones."
This is a place near Minions, where long-dead people built
monuments in pride, to show that they were house-dwellers
who knew law, instead of savage roadfarers who knew only
luck.

With Mark and Jidbell Cooper I walked among the stones,
where the people had built in pride—and wondered who the
people were. There is a lovely poem of Shelley's, *Ozymandias*,
which gives the say about the house-builders for all time. It is
of "two vast and trunkless legs of stone," standing in the middle
of a desert. There is an inscription:

> My name is Ozymandias, king of kings:
> Look on my works, ye Mighty, and despair!

In the last lines, quietly, the poet drives home the point that

there *aren't* any works to look on. "Nothing beside remains . . .

. . . The lone and level sands stretch far away."

On Minions Moor, and all over that part of Cornwall,
among the carved rocks, it is easy to appreciate Shelley's
poem. But easier still if a laughing young wagon-man and
his tawny sister move about among the stones that some few
thousand years ago were to mark the end of young wagon-
men and tawny road-girls.

Jidbell Cooper was full-grown and high-bosomed, with a
dark, smiling face and a clean line to her arms and legs. Black
hair came curling, not too cared-for, above her nearly black
eyes, and her teeth gleamed against the blackness of her eyes
and hair as she stood posed by one of the ancient stones, and
laughed at the dead men who built on Bodmin Moor.

Unable to read or write, she knew, beyond any book-lore
she knew, that the stones marked the passing of a challenge,
when road-life was deemed at an end and building was to be
all. Where some earlier Jidbell Cooper may have wept for
the passing of the old ways, she laughed in pleasure again,
and came down from the Mound to take me back to her
father's wagons.

There was tea by the fire when we got back, and old Phrania
Cooper gave a say about an ancestor of theirs, Garra Cooper,
who rode a race with death and reached his goal.

Garra had been told by a woman who could see things in a
crystal that he would die on a red-heather moor at the next
sunrise, by the hand of a woman who loved him. So out from
Cornwall, that land of red heather, he started hot-foot, on the
fastest horse that grazed by the Cooper wagons.

A hundred miles and more he rode that day, pushing his
horse without mercy as evening approached, because there
was red heather everywhere, and if night overtook him among
that heather then sunrise would follow, and death. Mile after
mile he raced, seeing no escape, until at last he came to the

upwaters of the Severn, and stood on a red-heather moor at nightfall, and saw a bare country on the farther bank, with not a heather plant for miles.

Twice he put his horse at the ford, but the Severn was in flood, and each attempt was a failure. But night was coming fast, and Garra knew the dawn must not find him in that place, so he drove the horse at the ford again, and over.

Then, at the farther bank, the tired horse slipped, but all was far from lost. Garra and his horse were swept away, down-river, for more than a mile, but horse and man were of the best, and they kept upright in the stream. Until in the black darkness of the night the horse was wedged between two rocks, with the water rising and Garra's feet trapped in the stirrups.

But all that was a song and a say of happiness compared with Garra's thoughts when the dawn came, and he saw he was back on the heather side of the Severn, like to be drowned even before the sun should rise to bring him death anyway.

The horse was dead, drowned struggling to the last, and the water was lapping under Garra's chin, when a voice came from the bushes by the river's brink. Into the water waded a tall and lovely girl, fighting against the stream, and clinging to a rope she had tied to the stump of a tree.

"But one minute," she panted. "But one minute, my tawny one, and I shall save you."

"Go back," screamed Garra. "Go back, and leave me to drown." Because the sun had come up behind the girl, and he could see love in her eyes, love tearing out the heart of her while she worked to save him.

The rest is a short say. She got the rope over Garra's shoulders, just at the second when the dead horse worked loose and was swept away. And the rope in her strong, loving hands brought Garra to the bank, strangled, as the sun rose full, and Garra had won his race.

We kept silent after that simple story of bad luck. The Coopers had heard it before, and I had heard it in many versions, the hard-luck stories of warfare and the sea. But it was easy to be more deeply impressed by Phrania's version, there on the moor at Minions, with the red heather round and the horses of a new Garra Cooper grazing near.

The little single-deck bus that goes from Rillamill to Liskeard had passed unnoticed while we gossiped and drank the tea. To walk over Caradon or across the moor was my only way home, and I was not in love with the prospect, since I had already walked most of the way from Menheniot. Garra looked at his granddaughter and nodded.

"The little black one," he instruced, and Jidbell rigged a small tent. There was pride in my stepping by their fire, for I knew I was more than forgiven when I was allowed to stay. From the opening of my tent, when we were settling down, I looked out at the edge of the moor, past the flicker of the fires, and was drunk with pleasure to think I was part of this scene.

"Good luck," I called, one by one to the family, as they went to tent or wagon. "Good luck," I called to Garra Dunnaha last, and all the grim humour of the tent-people came in reply.

"God bless," said Garra Dunnaha Cooper.

CHAPTER EIGHT

Huckleberry Finn

THE stoats," said young Tommity Cannadine, and peeped at me sideways, his dark brown eyes alert and watchful. "The stoats is terrible about here. Look at *that*."

He pointed to a little heap of feathers on the grass near his father's caravan. Then he waved towards a dead stoat, a few yards farther on.

He did *not* wave towards the huge poultry-farm near by; a farm whose boundary was the green disused lane in which the caravan stood. Stoats existed, in large numbers; there was one, dead. They killed chickens, even in the green lane; there were the feathers. Seven-year-old Tommity turned away with the air of one terminating a successful conference.

"Where's your father?" I inquired.

"Why?" asked Tommity.

He had seen me once, a year earlier, and it was in the highest degree unlikely that he had forgotten my face or voice. But he was offering no confidences. Why should he? I was a townsman.

"I wanted Simon for a minute," I said carelessly, taking care to use his father's first name. Tommity hesitated.

A big lurcher came from under the caravan, advancing inch by inch with a wicked show of teeth and a tiny menacing growl that was almost a purr. Ignoring him, I chatted carelessly with the boy, until the dog had sneaked near enough to get the scent of me and to remember our previous meeting. Then, when the lurcher had settled down, I turned to Tommity again.

Fortunately, I knew just what was going on in the boy's mind. He was alone in the green lane, except for the lurcher, but his main function was to pretend that the caravan, or at least the near-by fields, were full of the Cannadine.

If some prowling villager, who might pilfer a bridle or pail, came down the lane, Tommity would be the happy gipsy-child playing beside his caravan, with his father and his uncle and his elder brothers within call. If some hostile wagon-man, who might steal a horse or a set of harness, came the way, Tommity would identify him and the lurcher would mark him. While in the event of a visit from the poultry-farmer or a policeman, the innocent child was ready with his tale of the marauding stoats. I turned away up the lane.

"I'm just going to the top of this," I explained. "And then I'm coming back down this way again, to the main road. If your father shows up—don't waken him if he's asleep in the wagon—tell him my name. I'm Jim Phelan." I walked up the lane, and took care not to look back.

Half an hour later I came down the grass-grown road again. There had been several small changes by the Cannadine wagon.

On my earlier appearance a mare tethered on a long rope had been grazing at the junction of the green lane with the highway. The grass was better at that spot, but legally it would count as trespass, since any pedestrian would come too near the mare's heels. A couple of battered rusty bicycles had been lying near the caravan, and a big log lay half-way through a gap in a hedge, dropped in transit between the field and the green lane. All was different on my second visit.

The mare was now tethered some twenty yards up the green

road, on poorer pasture but in a strictly legal position. The old bicycles had disappeared, and the log was now lying in the lane, no longer the putative property of the man who owned the field. The heap of feathers was slightly larger, and the dead stoat was a few feet closer to it. Also, a tiny chicken-coop containing a live hen, obviously the lawful property of Simon Cannadine, now stood near the caravan, presumably to show any wayfarer how severely poor honest wagon-folk might suffer from the depredation of stoats.

In other words, the stage was set, in case I was a policeman in plain clothes, a town official with the right to ask questions, or a city snooper whose curiosity might be injurious. The stage was set, and the stage-manager was a seven-year-old boy.

I passed on down the lane without looking to right or left except for a nod to Tommity. The lurcher saw me to the main road and then went back.

No youngsters in the world have such a happy childhood as the wagon-children of Britain and Ireland. It is no wonder that they make powerful men and beautiful women.

Thrown on their own resources in their early years, chastised as roughly as a she-wolf's cubs, and caressed likewise, compelled to work from the age of six or seven, knowing little or nothing of play as it is known in the towns, acquainted almost from birth with darkness and hunger, with animals and men, living from hand to mouth on the edge of an always-new moor—these children might be pitied, and are in fact pitied, by anyone whose rule of life is taken from dusty books or printed forms.

Actually they live among, and work at, things only attainable in play by the children of a few very wealthy and very intelligent city people. Mark Twain has fixed the type for all time, in the character envied by generations of boys everywhere, Huck Finn.

The Cannadine wagon was in a lane by Garri Ghyll, where a loitering stranger would be noticed by many—noticed, above all, by Tommity Cannadine. So I waited in the pub at

Nenthead, with an occasional glance down the moor road, until I saw Simon Cannadine's wife coming down from a by-way.

Josia Cannadine (or Joyce, or Josie; no one ever knows how to spell names in wagons, the people concentrating on the sound) had the wide face and high cheek-bones, the long eyes and small mouth and red-golden colour which give many of the English wagon-people an American Indian appearance, and which told me her mother's name had been Brant or Colin. I said my name and business, told my mother's name, and mentioned Ireland. In a minute we were laughing together in praise of Tommity's shrewdness, as we walked down to the old green lane.

Josia had a little girl with her, one who would be tall. (All the Cannadine are tall, and have long, Scots-looking faces.) The child's name was Marla, and I went into talk about Marla Cooper and other Marlas I knew among the wagons. Josia was matter-of-fact about it. The girl's name was Marla because there was always a Marla Cannadine—that was all!

The youngster, on the other hand, was plainly impressed by the fact that her name was on the Cornish roads. One could almost see her counting Minions Moor as part of her heritage. I mentioned a doll I had seen at a toyshop in Lancaster—Marla asked how far did the horses stray on a moor in Cornwall.

Strictly business! Marla would be the person who went out on the moor behind Garri Ghyll to look for the horses when they strayed. Wherefore, if Cornwall *was* to be part of her territory—how big was a Cornish moor?

Simon Cannadine had only met me for a few minutes, far from the Border country, down near Small Heath beside Birmingham. But I had been in good company that night, with one of the Smiths from Hertford and two of the Norfolk Bakers to give me luck. So that Simon would accept me as entitled to sit by his fire.

At the same time, since I was a stranger and obviously more than half a houseman, he would offer no confidences. The question was—what did I *want* by his fire?

It is always thus when one of the gorgia—which means us, who live in cities—makes any approach to the wagon-people. Rightly, of course. (Imagine a wagon-man walking into a bank and commencing to ask questions about the bank-manager's parentage and religious beliefs!)

Thus the tripper or tourist looking for picturesque details in a gipsy-camp is likely to find them, at so much per detail. The luckless writer who says he is in search of a story is apt to hear one. Who is to blame if it is a story about the gipsy-man having served with distinction in the last War, or of the gipsy-woman's admiration for the Church of England service, or even a tale of a poor honest wagon-man having lost his last chicken because the marauding stoats were terrible?

Once, many years ago, I called in to see Victor Gollancz, a publisher for whom I have the most profound admiration. Since those days Victor has been thoroughly decent to me, as to many another writer, even and often of those who do not work for his publishing house. But at that time we had never met. I chanced to be in London, found myself passing his office, and went in to see Victor Gollancz.

I only wanted to say hello, and had no business whatever to discuss. But—could I fool that shrewd publisher into believing anything so unlikely! He knew many of my Irish friends, knew my own personal background, and was obviously waiting all the time for me to get to the point and ask him for something.

As far as I can remember, I finished up by borrowing twenty pounds. Or it may have been thirty. *Noblesse oblige!* I had to have a reason for calling, and I couldn't think of any other.

The same thing applies when a stranger goes to a wagon-fire. He had better want something, and know what he wants, and ask for it more or less directly. Also it had better be something the wagon-man understands. Otherwise there will be a say about how lovely the local parson's service is, or about the depredations of stoats.

What I wanted to know was whether, exogamy being the general rule between the Brants and the Cannadines, the women married into their husbands' wagons, or the men married into the girls' wagons, or both.

Anyone may imagine what would happen to a stranger who shot out such a question by a wagon-man's fire. There would be coshes in that say, as the Colins put it.

Wherefore I asked for a pup of the lurcher.

We dickered happily about the few shillings for the pup. I mentioned casually that I had been a tramp and had spent much of my life on the road. Simon froze. Wagon-people and tramps do not mix much, the two classes maintaining a kind of armed neutrality at best. But I mentioned that I got a few pounds for a story now and then, did not go the road any more—except occasionally to see my friends among the Smiths and Coopers and the rest. The dicker was resumed.

After I had had a can of tea I came round very carefully to Josia, Simon's wife. As I hoped, she admitted with some slight surprise that, as I had known, her maiden name had been Brant. Thereafter I quickly ran off the names of two or three Brants I knew, and breathed more easily. The exogamy explanation came later, casually, and with the assumption that I knew it already. There is no other approach to a wagon-say.

My chief interest in the question was because of the children. Tommity Cannadine sat by the camp-fire while I talked with his parents. Intently, with the tip of his tongue protruding, he sharpened a dozen short sticks to make pegs for snares. That object idolized by wagon kids, "a real genuwine Barber knife," flashed and glittered as his strong little hands turned the wooden stakes back and forward, whittling the square points into exactly the correct taper.

An intellectual millionaire might have paid ten dollars an hour to have his son allowed to play with Tommity.

On the other side of the fire, equally preoccupied, young Marla laboured. From each of three baskets she chose in turn a sprig of fern and a couple of wild flowers. A box near by held small gaudy artificial plants, to blend with the fern and make a background. Marla made the posies.

Those children were happy. I had seen thousands like them on the roads of England. But there were others, and I wanted to know why they existed, side by side with Tommity and Marla. The question about exogamy really led to the answer, but not in the way I had expected. It was very simple after all when it came, but there was every excuse for a townsman having missed it. The whole thing is a question of housing.

Just as there are slums in the cities, dirty, battered houses unfit for human use, so there are slums on the road. But, of course, it would never be apparent to a casual eye. One caravan looks like another from the outside. Yet I had seen, on the edges of Hertfordshire, in the Smith country, pale, sickly, miserable children beside caravans, children who had never known one day's happiness since their birth. Puny and vermin-ridden, covered with scabies, their little pale faces eaten alive with impetigo, they went the roads day after day, and rested from their work not to play but to scratch themselves.

Now these children were in wagons, and they were in Hertfordshire. Therefore it was long odds that their name was Smith. But I knew that Joyce Smith, the mort of Black Harry, would no more have had a group of those disease-eaten youngsters to play with her own bonny brood than I would have taken them home with me. How could such a state of affairs exist, among a people whose first rule is family friendship?

The slums. There are slums on wheels as well as in the streets. That is the answer.

Where a caravan is contaminated there is little or no chance of escape. That is, for poor people—and only poor people would let their wagon get dirty. Year after year and generation after generation the thing gets worse, until in the end it is not a caravan full of children with impetigo but a caravan full of impetigo with children in it.

It started in the latter half of the nineteenth century, at a time when the Poor Laws were being rigidly enforced against the road-folk. Death, accident, imprisonment, or other misfortune might come to the headman of a wagon. Thereafter that wagon-family would be impoverished.

Diseases like impetigo and scabies are trifling matters in a city. They happen, and they are eliminated in a few days. But in time of stress (during the London blitz, for instance), whenever many people slept together and passed on blankets or other bedding, such contagions spread fast and far. In ships and barracks and camps every doctor and quartermaster knows how difficult it is to keep scabies and impetigo in check.

Even then the soldier or sailor is only attacked for a few days. But for the people of the wagon-slum there is no escape. It would only take about five days, and would cost no more than thirty pounds, to fumigate everything and kill the diseases. But they never have the five days to spare, and they never have the thirty pounds. So there is no escape until they abandon the road, and drift to the slums of some town. (Having first sold their caravan to some townsman in search of romance!)

The wagon will be sold to a city man because no road-goer will buy it. Every caravan on the road is known, and, of course, the slum-wagons are marked out in the says, as surely as the street-slums are marked out on city maps.

At that point the question of exogamy has a bearing. It was the kind of thing a city writer would only stumble on by accident. I have often been glad I dickered for the lurcher pup with Simon Cannadine.

Exogamy among savage tribes will be familiar to many readers. The young people of two neighbouring or allied tribes marry one another instead of interbreeding. Roughly the same kind of thing happens among wagon-people.

There is no hard and fast rule. If a wagon-girl from the South of England does in fact want to marry into some caravan-clan in Scotland or Ireland there is nothing to prevent

G

her. At the same time circumstances generally limit the choice to two families.

Thus the Smiths and Bakers intermarry a good deal. There is already a well-marked Smith-Baker face, readily identifiable even by a city man who knows the two older families.

But immediately with intermarraige comes the property question. Manifestly a young man cannot ask a girl to marry him until he has a wagon or a share in a wagon, a tent to sleep in and a clan with whom to go the road. Any more than a bank-clerk can get married until he can offer his fiancée a house or a flat, a furnished room, or at least accommodation with his parents.

The girls go to the wagons of the men they marry.

Now, is the reader coming the road with me? Imagine a gathering of wagon-people, where trading and love-making and marriage-fixing are in progress. Imagine two men, with caravans precisely similar on the outside, making offers for the same girl.

There may be little or nothing to choose between the men physically. But the wagons! One is an ordinary caravan, from an ordinary clan like Harry Smith's or Charlie Baker's; one is a 'crabby wagon' known in a hundred says for three generations.

So—slum goes to slum, and the dirt holds its own.

The slum-wagons are a very small percentage of those on the road, and their owners have as little contact with the ordinary wagon-people as a slum-dweller from the East End of London has with the residents of the Savoy Hotel.

Besides, the road-folk themselves are driving the others off the road, in brutal fashion, but effectively and to good purpose. The owner of a dirty wagon is kept off a pitch. He takes the leavings of the villages and the roads, gets only the miserable dregs of the tatting-field. In time he gives up the hopeless struggle, sells his crabby wagon to a gorgio, and moves into a city.

Among the others, ninety-nine per cent., the children are

the healthiest and happiest in the world. Young Tommity Cannadine cannot read or write, will probably never learn, but since he was two years old he has played camp.

I told him about my own son, to see which things he would note. The fact that my boy could answer the telephone before he was two meant nothing. Telephones had no place in Tommity's life. Neither his father nor his mother had ever used one, and as far as he was concerned the tall poles with the wires on were some kind of fence. When he heard my boy could box he brisked up, and demanded details.

I tried to explain a boxing-tournament at a school. Thirty-two boys could engage, and the number be reduced, pair by pair, until the last two fought to see which one was the best of all the thirty-two. Tommity liked that.

But he explained very gravely that our system was unfair! Because the best boy would be tired "after all them fights," so that the last contest would not be a real fight at all. Promoters of school and army boxing have had the same problem for decades.

Then I said that my boy had built an elaborate toy boat, spending weeks on the work, and producing a perfect model yacht.

"To sail in?" asked Tommity. I explained that the ship would be too small.

"To nail over the door?" was the next query. (Wagon-people sometimes nail a small carving instead of the traditional horseshoe over the caravan door.) When I said that the boat was only to sail as a toy, and to look at, Tommity exchanged pitying glances with his sister and turned back to his snare-sticks.

We have a lot to learn. Or unlearn.

CHAPTER NINE

Glamour

ALL the winding roads of the world are lovely, and the lanes of Britain and Ireland will rank with the best. It will not be easy to find more pleasant places than the lonely small lanes that curve and twist among the fells, up near Garri Ghyll where I had left the Cannadine wagons, in the Border country, the end of England, the roof of the north.

From the path over Cold Fell a man can see things to make him feel tall as a giant and small as a beetle—which is the real magic of hill-viewing. It is a good thing to know, in one second of a far view, that the world holds such a store of vastly different prospects, and that life is not really the narrow grey groove one can think it at times in the lowlands.

Cold Fell is not a big hill—a couple of thousand feet or so, not much higher than Caradon, in Cornwall. But, like Caradon, it has much to offer the eye, can give a walker the view of miles in space and centuries in time. There are many ways of life within eye-range up on Cold Fell.

My own road led north and west, on a track that passed the highest spot of the fell and then dropped away to nothing. Somewhere along that track would be a Fay family, who would take a message to Torry John Fay when next they went north over Bewcastle Fells.

I had not seen Torry since I left him by Cannobie Fork, and I wanted to let him know that the scholars and the books were on his side in his story about the Fay paper and the road-roving king. "Fixing a say," Torry calls it, which is the road equivalent of editing and collating. There would be Fay tents on Cold Fell, and my message would go north on the correct road.

The edge of the fell looks out over the only patch of lowland on the Border, so that one can see far on a fine day. Away to the west is the smoke of Carlisle, and still farther distant the blue of the Solway Firth, while on very clear days there show up beyond the sea what look like the hills of a whole new continent, or the northern mountains of Ireland at least, but are really the small heights of Kirkcudbright.

North, and only a few miles away, are the Cheviots and the Border, while behind and a little westward four great stone whales, blunt-headed and blue, come eternally swimming from far away on a sea of mist—the giant mountains of the Lake District.

From up there, too, a man can see the road to Gretna Green, with the track from his feet leading down to it, so that he wants to go hot-foot and be over to Gretna by noon.

My own way was not for Gretna, but along the track over the Fell to meet one of the Fays, and then for the main road east, to be back by Newcastle-on-Tyne and the Great North Road. I sauntered lazily and at random, knowing that some Fay child would see me, or some Fay dog come barking, even if I could not see the tents or wagons in the heathery hollows.

The heather spread to right and left of the track, spangled and glamorous, luring a man to think he could walk but a few yards among the purple and the spangling to the Solway or across to Kirkcudbright. A wide spread of purple heather, when there is dew on it to catch the sunlight, gleams as if there were a million tiny lights in a mist, throws a veil over the eyes, and beckons into mystery and glamour.

We had been talking about glamour, back at Simon Cannadine's wagon by Garri Ghyll, using the word in the gipsy sense, and comparing it with its present-day meaning. Now I remembered the talk of the night before, and looked round in the purple mist that was not a mist, and smelt the fell, and knew this for glamour too, even in the gipsy way of saying it as well as our own.

It is to be hoped that no filmgoer will be shocked to know the origin and meaning of the word glamour. Because Simon Cannadine had summed up our talk about slum-caravans by giving a say about a lovely, healthy girl who had been lured into marrying a man from a crabby wagon.

"Put the glamour on her," he said, wrinkling his nose in disapproval, as if he referred to one of the acts and facts of life which people do not usually discuss. "Put the glamour on her, so that they were married, and took the tawny beautiful one to live in his pest-wagon." He spat.

On the opposite side of the fire Josia too wrinkled her nose. Putting the glamour, I knew, among wagon-people was counted as one of the things that sometimes happen, the things every married woman knows but does not talk about. Now I was out on the top of Cold Fell, filling my eyes with the purply light that was not a mist, filling my nostrils with the smell of the fell, and I knew I was having the glamour put on me.

It is a fact that any man may test and prove. On a wide heather-moor, especially at sunrise, the wayfarer will be intoxicated, as if there were heath-people plying him with seductive liquors. There is an aphrodisiac quality in the heather-smell and in the heather-feel which he will know at once, but will like because of his intoxication, and which will bring him to hurry knee-deep in the purple mist, searching for the seducer.

Among men and women, or women and men, or more often among men and horses, the wagon-folk call that process putting the glamour. Literally it means putting one's hand on a person or a horse, to make certain that one will be followed.

It is a long way already from the Hollywood idea of glamour. But still near enough. One may read a few Hollywood divorce-reports and agree that it is still near enough!

To glam or glawm a person, especially a girl, is to fondle her intimately—to 'paw her about,' as we say in the cities. The glawmer is really the hand—but only the hand when used in this way. Putting the glamour on a male horse was a general practice in the days when horse-stealing was common. It is almost unused nowadays, except in places like Exmoor or the New Forest, where there are wild or nearly wild ponies.

In such a place, where most of the ponies are of little value, the wagon-man who can get a sturdy young stallion to follow him right into his camp will still be earning an easy week's pay in an hour or so. The simplest way is to put the glamour on the horse.

Back at his camp the wagon-man will have a clean young filly, alert and lively, and in the right state of mind and body to be thinking of sturdy young stallions on moors. He glawms the filly, rubs his clothes on her, strokes her all over, fondles the intimate parts of her body, feels the electric stirring of life in her, and then goes away. Without washing his hands, he goes in search of the wild-horse troop.

Standing up-wind and at a distance, he waits until the leader of the troop raises his head to look about him, pawing the ground and smelling at the breeze like a wayfarer on a heather-moor at sunrise. When the wild horse has seen him the wagon-man moves, very slightly, waiting. Presently the horse comes, foot by foot, to sniff at the hand held out to him. Then the wagon-man moves a little more, brushing his hands on his clothes, letting the horse get accustomed to the smell of him, and then he walks slowly away. The horse follows.

That is the most practical form of putting the glamour. A thousand stories of gipsy magic with horses, stories generally made and told by city people, are based on the practice. There are other applications of the principle which need not be discussed here. Every one knows them really, but the suburban housewife and Josia Cannadine will both wrinkle their noses slightly and leave them undiscussed.

Now we are a long way from the filmgoer's idea of Hollywood glamour. But perhaps not so far from Hollywood itself!

So I laughed at myself on the top of Cold Fell, when I knew I was being glamoured by the heather-scent, knew that the moor was glawming me with her scented hands and clouding my eyes with mistiness made from the twinkle and spark of dewdrops on purple heath. I laughed at myself, and went on down the path, until I saw a green wagon and two black tents in a hollow, and went over to talk with the Fays.

A vicious heavy-weight dog, half collie and half greyhound —a wicked breed—shot out from behind the tents and raced at me silently. I stood him off with the blackthorn I carried, and waited to see whether I must fight him down, or if some one would come. Tinker dogs are always at their most vicious when left on guard alone, and I knew there would be no one in the tents.

The dog was beginning to circle me, silently and watchful, and I thought at last I must kick him under the chin to make my peace. (It is a hurt no dog can stand, not even a fighting mastiff.) He was coming in for my legs, and I had my right foot drawn back, when a voice called from the upper end of the hollow.

The dog crouched down, and I passed him. A girl was coming down the slight incline into the dell where the tents were, and we met in the middle of the hollow. This was a Fay, I could see at one glance, and I made no hesitation about giving the show-out sign, the open-hand-at-shoulder greeting of the wagon-people.

"Good luck, sister," I said, and told my name. "Cannadine Simon told me I might meet your people this way."

She was nearly of my own height, all the Fays being big people, although not as tall as the Cannadine of the Border.

Her face was browner than usual, even among her black family, and she had marvellous teeth that gleamed out against the black of her eyes when she smiled.

She wore a faded, thin, light blue frock, tied at the middle with a ragged red sash, and seemed to have little else on except her shoes. The frock was short, and her well-shaped brown legs were bare, as were her arms. Three fresh rabbit-skins dangled in her left hand, and she snatched them away from the dog as she stood smiling and waited for me to say more.

It was clear from the first moment that she knew I was a gorgio. But my behaviour with the dog, and my having put the Cannadine surname first, wagon-fashion, had obviously convinced her that I was at least some one who knew how to approach a camp-fire. But I could see that my name meant nothing to her, and I was bitterly disappointed.

Then I mentioned Torry Fay, and in a moment she had identified me. She led the way to the fire beside the tents.

We lay by the fire, and talked while a tin can boiled to make tea. Wagon-dwellers of any race never sit at a fire, but lie on their sides, or stretch chest downward with both elbows on the ground. It is a leisurely, pleasant, and intimate position for a fireside talk, very difficult at first for a city man, but luxurious in time.

"I should have known you," the girl said, laughing. "Fay Michael, Torry's young brother, is always talking about you. To hear Michael a person would think you and him had bought all the city of Cardiff, and stolen the ships out of the sea." She propped herself on one elbow, and turned mocking black eyes on me.

"Michael," I said very gravely, "is a man who knows good people when he meets them. Who am I to say he was wrong about me?" I met her black eyes, and mocked them back. "Three weeks ago," I told her, "on Minions Moor in Cornwall, I had talk with Jidbell of the Coopers. Now *there* is a bright, quick, tawny girl," I continued, "who listened to the say about Michael and me, in the coal-steamer out of Cardiff, that had rifles in the coal and fetched up in an Irish port by accident and——"

"Silent Jem," she laughed. "Poor, silent, quiet Jem, who never says one word for himself. Your mother must——" She broke off, and got up to make the tea, then lay down again when it was poured into tin cans.

"Where are all your people?" I asked, when we had rolled cigarettes. "And what do they call you, black one?"

"The women in Penrith. The men out on the Fell," she told me. "There's a dip across to the west, with two big warrens, and we're putting in a week on the rabbits for Penrith market before we go on for the Wall and Bewcastle." She paused, and lit her cigarette with a twig from the fire. "They call me Grania," she finished, after a short hesitation.

This was one of the cases where I was glad I had read a book or two. I knew exactly what was in Grania's mind, and the reason for her hesitation.

Wagon-people neither know nor care anything about the way a name is spelt—any more than Shakespeare did. They get the sounds right, but will sometimes be led into pronouncing a name wrongly, by force of suggestion, even when they know they are making a mistake. Many wagon-girls, for instance, are called Aphrodite, but in time the name tends to become Dytie or Affrytie, which might sound like 'dirty' or 'affrighted.'

Grania did not like her name. Because it sounded like grannie and would sometimes be pronounced that way—she herself not knowing how or whence the name arose. Since I liked her mocking smile, I was glad of the few books.

"Grania," I repeated. "Now here's another Fay name out of the past. Michael is always boasting that his people were the kings of Ireland—before the Irish got there. And Torry will have it that a wagon-man of the Fays was a king in Scotland—before there were either kings or wagons. Now here you turn up on the top of Cold Fell with the name of an Irish queen on you."

Grania laughed, but I could see she was eager to hear more. I told her that Grania was really the Irish word for Grace, a woman's name, and I was telling her about Grania Umaile, or Grace O'Malley, a pirate queen from Galway Bay who came all the way to the court of Queen Elizabeth in London, and sailed home in her own ships with gifts from the English monarch. But in the middle of the telling the dog barked, and a little group of people turned in off the track into the hollow.

A solid, black-looking man, for all the world like Torry Fay, came first, with two lurchers by his heels and a big sling of snares and nets over his shoulder. Two tall young men, obviously his sons, walked slowly about eight feet behind one another, with a long stick carried between them on their shoulders. From the stick hung about two-score rabbits, and a boy of about fifteen who came behind had rabbits hanging all round him, from his shoulders and his pockets, from his belt and in his hands. A white-haired man brought up the rear, with two ferret-bags in his hands and a shotgun hanging behind him.

"More work," said Grania, grimacing. "I'll have no finger-tips left from skinning rabbits by the time we hit Bewcastle Fells." I stood up and signed peace to the Fays.

The fact that I had been lying by the fire, drinking tea with Grania, seemed to eliminate the need for any question. Grania's father nodded and threw down the nets, then lay by the fire and reached for a tin of tea. I threw him a cigarette and told my name.

"Good luck," he said at once. "We hear about you from Torry. And Michael," he added, with a smile at his daughter. I sensed that I had been pretty thoroughly discussed in that family before ever I came to their fire.

The young men and the stripling had unloaded their cargo of rabbits, and the old man was putting the ferrets away under the wagon. One by one they came to the fire, reaching out eagerly for tins of tea and cigarettes.

The boy was shy, and called me sir when I threw him a city

cigarette instead of the dust-scrap smoke he had started to make. Grania's father and her brothers watched me quietly, waiting. The girl herself had even more mockery than before in her smile.

It was a decisive moment. The stranger who is called sir by a wagon-man and accepts the word might as well cut his throat for all the hope he has of ever again finding friendship by a camp-fire.

"What's this?" I demanded of the boy's father, laughing roughly. "In the cities a flunkey or a taxi-driver will call me sir. But I never thought to hear the word by a didicai fire, let alone among the black Fays. What's this?" I shouted angrily. "Am I to be treated like a gorgia gentleman, among Torry's people?" I pretended to get up from the fire.

The small incident established my position at once, and there was no more politeness. In a minute we were discussing the stories of Michael Fay, who had been a gun-runner for the I.R.A. years earlier. The young fellow grinned, and hastened to talk about dogs and ferrets—which is the wagon equivalent of an apology.

Grania and her father gossiped about Michael's brushes with the law, and asked no questions about my business by their fire. Only when I rose to leave did I mention the message for Torry Fay.

Grania repeated it after me, her lips moving inaudibly. Then she recited it aloud, getting the exact rhythm of my speech and putting the emphasis as I had done. It is the wagon equivalent of having a verbatim shorthand note taken, and I knew Torry would receive it as spoken, even if it came to him at second or third hand.

Then Grania and her young brother walked with me to the top of the hollow. The wicked mongrel accompanied us, never once relaxing, although he no longer growled or showed his teeth.

On the lip of the dip the two Fays and the dog halted, and I turned for the track towards the Newcastle road. When

Grania heard I was going to Newcastle-on-Tyne she hesitated for a moment, then gave me a say for one of the Packers, whose wagons would be coming from Newcastle towards Hexham. It was only a short say—four sentences—but I felt as pleased as if I had been given a valuable present.

The fact is that the wagon-folk wrongly regard us of the cities as unreliable, selfish, and viciously indifferent to another person's need or suffering. To them the fact that a townsman will hurry to a telephone in order to report a road-accident, or will write a letter of introduction for a friend about to travel, means nothing at all. As far as the road-people are concerned, when a house-dweller is in trouble his friends pass by on the other side.

Of course, there is much to be said for their point of view. But, also of course, we are by no means as indifferent and heartless as they think. Only the use of telephone and post-office do not register as aids for the unfortunate in the view of wagon-people. Their own first reaction is to inquire what is wrong, and their second question is always—who does the other person want told? A case occurs to me which will clarify the difference of outlook.

In a lane near Berkhamsted one day I came on a family of the Careys, whose caravan had been burnt the night before. Practically everything they owned in the world had been destroyed. An ancient man and woman, with their four adult children, sat by the roadside, after a night spent out of doors in the rain, waiting to send a message to some of their people. They knew me when I spoke, and realized that I wanted to help. But they did *not* know that my ideas of help were practical.

Their people were in Kent, "somewhere Tonbridge way." They were in Berkhamsted, about fifty miles as the crow flies, two hours distant by telegram, one night's journey for an ordinary letter, three minutes by phone.

But it was at least two days' travel for a wagon-family, apart from the fact that London was in between. So the family waited for one of the Colins from Kent to come along. He would carry a message for them, carry some of their people, and in two or three days the help would come and all would be well.

I asked where I could phone their relatives in Kent. They stared.

Then I inquired if they knew a stopping-place of their people, anywhere near a village post-office, so that I could wire. They looked blank.

Presently I had a bright idea. If they knew even roughly where their people were—on which side of Tonbridge—I could telephone the police and have a message written down, to be handed over to one of the wagon-folk. At the mention of the police the old couple looked black, and immediately muttered that everything was all right now—they weren't really in any trouble after all.

In the long run I did manage to extract the name of a pub near which the Careys would almost certainly be camped in a lane for the midday halt. Half an hour later I was back beside the burnt caravan with the message delivered.

That success saved my face with the old couple. But it did not convince them that civilized methods were best, since they regarded my establishment of contact as a pure fluke. (Which, of course, it was.) The correct method was to wait for one of their tribe to 'carry a say.'

Now Fay Grania was entrusting me with an obviously intimate say on the edge of Cold Fell. Here was the other side of the picture. Rightly I felt proud.

The girl hesitated a little, moved a few feet away from her brother, and looked at me again after I had repeated the message and mimicked her intonation. Then she came as near to flushing as a wagon-girl may, and laid a hand on my arm.

"It is a hurry-say, Jem," she explained. "Big for *me*. There will be a wagon-meet outside Newcastle this week," she went on slowly. "And there is a girl of the Baillies that Tolly Packer might see—if he does not get my say."

"He gets it to-night," I reassured her. "I shall be hitch-hiking, and for me Newcastle is only a few hours away, not two days." Grania looked doubly pleased, and reached a hand into the breast of her frock.

"Then put the glawmer on Tolly for me," she laughed, and ran her open hand down my face, slowly from my eyes over my nose and mouth. "And give him *that*." She passed me a scrap of folded cloth, like a small sewn envelope, and turned swiftly away with her brother.

Walking on down the track, I put the little envelope away. It had the same scent as the girl's body, as her hand. Clearly it was a "hurry say," indicating a greater urgency than might be attributed to the Baillie girl. It was the glamour, in the horse-copers' sense, in the original sense, and up there on Cold Fell I was back to Hollywood fundamentals after all.

CHAPTER TEN

The Say of the Raggady Rawnie

ABOVE Stonebridge, in Warwickshire, only a few miles from the city of Birmingham, there is a small heather-grown patch of wasteland. From time immemorial it has been a meeting-place, twice yearly, for the wagon families who live on the road.

Anywhere from Cornwall to the Scottish Border, at some time or other a family wrangle, or an involved trade-discussion, among wagon-people will be postponed with the phrase "Good luck, then. We'll see what they say at the small heath." The meeting is a kind of rough parliament, and the centuries-old name survives, even on postcards and bus-tickets—"Small Heath, nr. Birmingham."

The gathering on the small heath is first of all concerned with wagon-routes and family trades—or changes of trade. Next in order of importance come quarrels about property —horses and wagons, lucrative tatting-pitches, "right of way" through another family's territory, and so on. The arrangement of marriages also is in many cases completed "at the small heath."

There is a good deal of fighting besides, regular high-class ring-battling, for horses or harness or girls who cannot make up their minds. And invariably after the main business of each day the giving of says goes on by the fires.

The old women come into their own at such a time. It is publication day, the première of their own film, the first night of their own drama. The old women give the say, note the quickened breath and avid attention of their hearers, and are pleased as the playwright or author is pleased.

Consider, then, the predicament of Ma Mella Scampe, compelled for nearly ten years to keep silent or nearly so, when all the time she knew one of the best says that had ever been given. Mella knew the say, but dare not tell it because the telling would have meant an end, would have meant that there was no say of the Raggady Rawnie. So she kept quiet.

The Raggady Rawnie every one knew. Up and down the roads, for years after the first big war, the wagon-folk knew her, and got used to her graceful side-gliding walk. Also they knew her quickness of eye and tongue, that would talk silver money out of a gorgia pocket while another wagon-girl might go empty-handed. With the wagons of the Lorrekers the Raggady Rawnie travelled, not mated with any of the travelling-men but riding the road on her own.

Some said it was from the top-highlands of Scotland she came, and some from West Ireland, because there was a kind of Gaelic in her tones, although she knew romani well enough with the words nearly right. And Tamaro Colin, who had been in Barcelona, swore she must be a Spaniard or from some country east of Spain, because she had wagon-words that only the old people knew in England.

Be that as it might, the Raggady Rawnie told neither one thing nor the other, but if she had come from Nottingham the day before then she said she came from Nottingham, and if from Carlisle she said Carlisle. So, since people on wagon-wheels are not paid for asking questions, then none of the road-people asked the Lorrekers further.

But the others, the towny-men with printed papers, and

H

the police, and the office-folks who gave the paper forms to fill in for even food-rations and identity and the like—*they* asked questions in plenty. Especially just after the first big war, when every one everywhere was questioned if they moved, let alone people going the road in a wagon.

For such, since they had the right and the power to ask, with the law and the gaol-house to back their asking, the Raggady Rawnie gave her say, as she had to do. And she showed her papers, as she had to show them, however black and shame-like the papers would make things.

The Raggady Rawnie had been in a lunatic asylum before the end of the First World War. That was the story she could not hide when the officials and the police would compel her to show her papers.

For the rest, she spoke to no one, or to few except Lilygay Lorreker, the eldest daughter of the family, or to Lilygay's brothers. And occasionally, when their wagon-roads crossed, to Ma Mella Scampe. Mella was Lilygay's great-great-aunt, a hundred or more, who had earned silver money by the hundredweight as a circus-rider, right across Europe, in her young days.

Every one else got pleasant, soft, short phrases, with a kind of Gaelic tone in them, from the Raggady Rawnie. And she went the road with the Lorreker wagons for just over ten years.

There was always a many-side say, and no real word, as to how the Rawnie came first to the Lorreker fires. Some gave it one way, others gave it otherwise, but no one knew fact. Except that one day the police from Bury St Edmunds, in East Anglia, had handed the Raggady Rawnie over to the Lorrekers, and made them keep her because she was their kinswoman.

They were wild times in the quiet East Anglian country, those days by the end of the First World War. Big soldier-camps were everywhere, since it was a lonely place with much heath and moorland. English soldiers and Scots, with

Americans and foreigners from Finland and Poland and places farther, crowds of artillery-men in big gun-parks, far away from the towns in the lonely lost parts of the countryside—a mixture of men was in East Anglia that year.

Naturally there would be trouble, with so many different breeds of men, all out in the heathlands and on the waste ground among the woods. Especially by the end of a big war, when men for years had grown accustomed to shooting and death, when there was violence and often plain murder among those in or out of the armies, especially the foreign men from the European soldiers, who were little used to the English way, the quiet way, of doing things.

That much came shouting from the headlines one day, when a Polish soldier shot his officer and took to the woods of East Anglia, with a rifle and a hundred rounds of ammunition. Six weeks it was before they caught him, after a dozen gun-fights with police or soldier-parties, in the lonely woods and black tangled thickets that were up and down East Anglia then as now.

There had been several such brushes, with men who had committed some crime or escaped from the camp-gaols and gone on the run in the woods, armed and desperate. But that six weeks' affair, with its succession of gun-fights, was the most serious for the wagon-people, since they were watched and halted and questioned everywhere while the runaway soldier was at large.

Then when he was captured there was quiet for a while, although there were other runaways in the woods. Until one night when the Lorreker wagons were camped in an old green lane by Assington Thickets, a matted wood where a steam-roller could hardly advance, let alone a man.

The wagons were in the lane on the wood-edge, and it was dark during a cloud-over of the moon, when two shadowy figures going up towards the Lorreker fires were halted by a man who stepped out of the wood with a rifle.

"Stand," he said, in a low, pleasant voice. "Make one sound and you will dead mans be."

A cackle of high-pitched laughter answered him, and he raised the rifle. Then he lowered it as the moon came from behind a cloud.

"More than a rifle you'll need, to make either of *us* a dead man," laughed a mocking voice, to add a second later, "Come on, boy, speak up. Speak up. What do you want on our road?" It was old Ma Mella Scampe, with Lilygay Lorreker, going up to the gipsy camp on their way back from Sudbury.

The man lowered the rifle still more, and came towards them. He did not laugh. But he was trying to laugh, as Lilygay and the old woman could see. Only his face was strained and set, even in the part-light of the moon, and the laugh would not come.

"Men, I thought, and enemies," he said apologetically. "Give luck to me, sisters. For the wood is black and I must die before they take me."

He said it all in a quiet, soft, pleasant voice that old Mella and Lilygay found very sad. So they pushed closer into the darkness of the wood-edge and asked him why he must die rather than be taken.

From Poland he came, and his name was Zolian. There was a little gathering of Polish soldiers, under their own officers in camp-huts, and Zolian's bad luck was to have as his officer a man who had been his wicked and vicious enemy in his own country. Zolian was only a circus-rider, and the other was a landowner, so there was not much chance for the circus-man when it was one man's word against another's.

So three times Zolian had been in prison in Poland. Each time, he swore there on the edge of Assington Thickets, each time for nothing but the sworn lies of his enemy, who hated him because a girl had smiled on the circus-rider instead of himself.

Then it looked as if the landowner would destroy Zolian outright, but the coming of the War saved things, and Zolian went away in the soldiers. Only—four years later, in far-away East Anglia, in England, who turned up as Zolian's officer but the same landowner, his bitter and vicious enemy?

Well, one persecution and one torment followed another, until the officer had Zolian awaiting a court-martial, for insolence and for attempting to strike him. A strange mix the Poland Army was in those days, according to Zolian. Because when Zolian was taken to the camp gaol the officer in charge was the same landowner again. It was double torment now, and at last the man had Zolian fixed, safe to be gaoled for years because he had struck an officer twice.

Gloating over Zolian, after giving him a kick or two, the man was, when the circus-rider, mad-desperate now, grabbed the rifle from a guard, shot the officer—dead, he hoped—and made it to the woods. Now he must die in the woods, fighting, for if they took him back he would be hanged anyway. And all because a Pole-girl far away liked the circus-rider best.

For Lilygay and Ma Mella it all sounded a most high fair say, there in the gloom by the wood-edge. But there was nothing they could do for Zolian, however much they might be sorry for his quiet voice and his pleasant way of saying he would shoot them dead.

"My say is this, Pole soldier," said Lilygay at last, and stood up to confront the stranger. "Throw away that gun and take the road. Find work on a farm and say you come from Wales. From Wales, mind. It is a country. They talk strange. Like you do. Do that, and stop this fool work of waiting with a gun to fight a whole army."

"Have no coat on," instructed Ma Mella, "and carry a log of wood on your shoulder. Or a forkful of hay, if you can find a pitchfork, and you can walk from here to Scotland unmolested." The two wagon-women began to turn away.

"It may be not," said Zolian sadly. "To-morrow and after they will send descriptions and photographs everywhere. So I must die here, presently. Then good-bye, sisters, and bushil-a-krim."

Now the last three words told Ma Mella and Lilygay that somewhere or other Zolian had lived in a wagon, or was a wagon-man himself. Because in mispronounced fashion he came near to saying the romani equivalent of "God bless you."

Then they considered what he had said about being a circus-rider, and suddenly old Ma Mella began to moan low to herself. Because she would have it that Zolian was kin of her own, a long way off and a long time back, since her circus-riding days all up and down Europe. Now here he was to be shot on the edge of a wood in Suffolk. Zolian her kin.

Lilygay too had been watching and listening closely enough, all through, to start when the Pole-man gave them the bushil-a-krim at the end. She fronted up to Zolian, as tall as himself, and looked deeply in his eyes, with the moonlight behind her.

"There is a brake of brambles twenty yards behind you and to the right," she said quietly. "You must sit in the heart of it and never move. Even if you hear soldiers and people searching. Then if you are shot—well, you are shot, and good-bye, Zolian. But if otherwise then you will hear from Mella or myself. I am Lilygay Lorreker."

So Zolian crept back into the brake of briars, and Lilygay went on to the wagons with old Ma Mella. But there was no word by the wagon-fires about what happened at Assington Thickets, neither that night nor for long.

Then the next morning, and for days afterwards, there was hot hue and cry round Suffolk after the Pole soldier who had shot his officer. The landowner was dead, and Zolian would be hanged. But there was little search by Assington Thickets, for the hue and cry had gone on to the woods near Bury St Edmunds, where a man like the runaway had been seen twice by night.

Although some said that man was only a gipsy poacher. One of the Lorreker clan, maybe.

But even round Bury St Edmunds the excitement faded after a few days, and the interest went to a better story still. For instead of a man it was a woman they picked up in the woods, a wild woman, walking stark mad down a woodland track towards the main Bury road.

Stark mad she was, and nearly stark naked, dressed in nothing but half of a ragged old patchwork quilt. Wearing a high head-dress like a crown, made from her own hair plaited with thin straw ropes, she walked down out of the woods, with the country people terrified even to ask her a question.

She had no words, except two. Raggady Rawnie, she said when a village policeman asked her name, and Raggady Rawnie was all she said when they led her away, and covered her nakedness, and put her in the hospital in Bury St Edmunds. With her strange tall hair-and-straw crown pointing up from her head, and with the ragged quilt round her, she was indeed a story and a person to remember.

Only two days the strange woman stayed in the hospital, long enough for the doctors to know she was a normal woman in every way except in her mind, and then she went to the lunatic asylum, blank and staring and strange as when she first walked out of the woods. There was no name for her except Raggady Rawnie, so on all the doctors' papers, and the mad-house certificates, and the printed forms of the police and the hospital, she was Raggady Rawnie, a wandering mad-woman, found in the woods outside Bury St Edmunds.

For a whole week there was no word from her, and no change in her mad, empty stare. Then for a second week the doctors questioned her, with no result except that they guessed she was a wagon-woman, from the brown of her arms and legs and the out-of-doors look of her empty, staring face. So the police went scouring again, among wagon-people from far and near, to see whose was the lunatic woman who had been deserted by the roadside.

Then by the third week the doctors said she was cured and not mad. She was to be discharged, to go back to her family. But who her people might be there was no saying. Until from the police came in word of a wagon-family, the Lorrekers, camped in the woods beyond Sudbury, who at last had to admit that the woman was theirs.

So, still a bit blank and staring, the woman called Raggady Rawnie was certified sane, and the Lorrekers had to accept her, since that was the law.

Of course, the Lorrekers did not fall over themselves to welcome a woman that looked mad, even if the doctors said she was sane. But they took her into their wagons, because they had to take her, with her papers to tell the shameful story that she came from the lunatic asylum, and that she had no fixed residence but lived in a wagon. "Address: n.f.r. Caravan Lorreker," was all the papers had to say, but it was enough in law to make the family liable for the woman called Raggady Rawnie.

So, up through the little village street she went, with her hair-and-straw crown still pointing up to the sky, and with Ma Mella Scampe walking softly beside her, keeping near. She had a few more clothes on now, and shoes, but she still wore the ragged patchwork quilt slung over her shoulders like a highland plaid. An outstanding figure was the Raggady Rawnie, a person to remember, even without her papers. Up to the Lorreker wagons she went, on the edge of the wood, and was peaceful for a while.

But already next day the villagers of Assington stared, when Raggady Rawnie came down the little village street again, with Ma Mella Scampe pressing close by her on one side and Lilygay Lorreker keeping near her on the other. Because even a village child could see she was not right, the tall woman with the hair-and-straw crown and the rag-patch quilt, who stared blankly ahead and walked slightly sideways.

It was a long time before the Lorrekers let her go out alone. But by then the police for miles round knew her, and there was no danger of her being lost in the woods again. Sad it was, sad near to make weeping, to see her so proud to show her papers—the papers that proved she was not mad now. A sad woman was the Raggady Rawnie, but people were kind, even the police.

Then the Lorrekers drifted north and west, slowly, into their own country of Derbyshire, because the war was over by that time and people could go the road again. Again the Raggady Rawnie came to be known, to officials and police in the Lorreker country, with her poor treasured paper to prove she was sane. Year by year she got better, and could talk silver money from a stranger anywhere, with the soft, slow speech and the deep, dark, honest eyes to convince him. But she never married or mixed with the Lorreker men, being close friends only with Lilygay, and with Ma Mella when she came the way.

That way it went for nearly ten years, with peace and pleasure for the Rawnie and the Lorrekers, except twice when there was shame and trouble for other cause. Anyone will know that a wagon-girl cannot live loosely like a girl in a city, and will know that chance-children belong among the houses instead of in the caravans. But the Lorrekers knew shame, twice, when Lilygay came to belly-swell, and named no wagon-man and took no husband, but each time had her chavo in her own wagon and answered the questions of no one but Ma Mella.

Seven years old one of Lilygay's boys was, and five years the other, when one day Lilygay came back from Colchester market to find ruin and death on the road where her family should have been. Two big motor-lorries had crashed into the wagons on the Colchester road, wrecking the caravans, crippling Ma Mella, and killing the Raggady Rawnie outright.

Then Lilygay knelt by the dead body and cried her eyes dry; kissed the dead face, and sobbed out the story. For, of course, the Raggady Rawnie was her husband, Zolian the Pole, wanted for murder, and hiding for ten years—hiding amid the police, with his stamped and signed papers to prove he was not a madwoman, but *had* been.

There had been only one way for Lilygay to save him. Disguise alone would not have served—he had to have an identity, a certified and guaranteed identity as a woman. At one time and another throughout the years Lilygay's brothers and uncles and cousins had had to prove, with their papers and otherwise, that they were not the long-hunted Pole. The Raggady Rawnie had only proved she was sane.

There had been no question of *her* being Zolian the Pole. There were her papers, to prove everything about her, including the fact that she had been in a lunatic asylum.

So the Raggady Rawnie had gone the road in safety for ten years, in the identity Lilygay had created out of nothing except a doctor's certificate, a plaited straw headdress, and the mind-quickness of a woman in love. Lilygay herself had gone to the hospital and the asylum, long enough to get the papers, and then to have the woman called Raggady Rawnie forced on the Lorrekers by the police.

Then, with the straw crown and the patch-quilt to identify the madwoman, all Assington or all Suffolk would have sworn that the woman who walked up to Assington Thickets with Ma Mella was the same woman who walked down with Mella and Lilygay.

It is one more story of a loving woman's wit, the story Ma Mella had to leave untold for ten years, even with her mouth watering at the say-give on Small Heath, until the need was past and poor soft-voiced Zolian was free from fear.

CHAPTER ELEVEN

The End of Rogue Enderley

MANHOOD and frankness and freedom from malice are found on the road as among the houses. Honesty of purpose and straightforward dealing are as common in the green lanes as in the towns. No less—and no more.

He would be mad who thought that every wagon-dweller was a frank and manly son of nature, mad to think that a person cannot be mean and crooked, and cowardly cunning, just because he lives above wagon-wheels.

The rogue elephant is driven out from the herd, but remains a rogue. In the towns it is not always easy to drive a rogue away. (For he may be a millionaire, or an aristocrat, or even one of the men who fill in the printed forms about driving away rogues!)

Likewise, on the road, even against the forest-cunning of a whole tribe, a rogue will now and then survive, by sheer wickedness and resource of wickedness. Boar Enderley survived for nearly fifty years.

In those five decades—or in four of them, since he was ten years old—Boar Enderley spread pain and misery and fear up and down the North Wales Road which was the Enderley run, first among the children of his own age, then among growing girls and stripling boys, then with his own wives and children or the wives and children of others.

Big and strong, swift with his eyes and hands—and feet—he was deadly in a fight as a boy. Manhood and mercy and good-fellowship are more common among boys than among men, in the wagons as in the houses. But young Boar Enderley knew nothing of them. When he got a boy down that boy was maimed.

Later, as a stripling, when he could box and wrestle with the best, even then the mean villainy of him came always uppermost in a fight. Where another would send a straight left to a chin, Boar Enderley flicked a crooked-nailed thumb to gouge an eye instead, or jabbed an elbow at the soft middle parts.

Of course, no wagon-crowd standing round a fight will tolerate such things for long. Twice on Small Heath the Boar came near to his end, after he had mauled two youths in the boxing-ring. Then he got cunning, and always after that the maiming or the dirty wound or the vicious underblow was an accident, or looked like one.

From those days came all the Boar's acts and practice of later years. Whatever villainy he did was always an accident, even by the romani rule of those who knew he was a rogue, and certainly by the law of the housemen, more concerned about explanations than facts.

When he took Livvea Calleran for his mort, him little more than seventeen, it was the same story. Anyone will know that a romani boy cannot marry unless he has a wagon or part of one. And a boy of seventeen will have no part.

But it so happened that Lemuel Enderley, the Boar's father, was drowned in the lake at Balla, by Frongoch, up in the Welsh mountains, so now young Boar had a fourth of a wagon, sharing with his three brothers, all older than himself.

Three weeks later, on the Holyhead Road, a stallion kicked Jaybird Enderley, the eldest brother, smashing his skull to a pulp and making the Boar's share one-third of a wagon. The mark of the stallion's shoe was plain on the dead man's face for the police and the coroner to see, and the coroner's jury gave sympathy to the bereaved family, as they say in towns.

But all up and down the North Wales Road every one knew Lemuel Enderley would not slip in a lake. And every one knew that a horseshoe can be used like a battleaxe, at the end of a club, and then nailed back on the horse's hoof for the police and coroners to see.

But, of course, no one gave a say to the plastramengros, the housemen's police, for what good would it do? So the Boar had a third of a wagon, and could get married.

By then some few began to call him Rogue Enderley on the roads. But that would be among themselves. In his presence, by a pitch or at a wagon-meet, men kept silent, and the Rogue kept silent too, watching those round with hard, mean, cruel eyes, turning always the cold, small smile for any word that to another man would mean offence and a hot-blood challenge.

When Dirk Enderley fell thirty feet into the hold of a cattle-steamer at Birkenhead, down among the trampling, panic-mad animals, he did not die, but was crippled for life, and could go the road no more. His one-third share of the wagon went to the Rogue, for little money and less luck, and Bantle Enderley, the remaining brother, knew fear.

Bantle Enderley, who would back a four-year-old unbroken stallion, or fight any two men on the North Wales Road—he had fear, and sold his share of the family wagon to the Rogue at the buyer's own price.

So it came on that although he was but nineteen the Rogue had been two years married to Livvea Calleran, and had a kushti vado—a fine family wagon—all for himself and his mort and his chavos. Two chavos there were by that time, fine, powerful younglings that came more of Livvea than of their father, and those two knew fear and pain, from their earliest days, to grow up with them.

Fear and pain were Livvea's too, through the years, but she loved the Rogue through it all, as women will, and loved her two fine growing sons, the pride of her eyes. Even when the Rogue took another girl in the wagon Livvea kept silent, and forgot it all when the girl had run away. But for weeks after the run-away she walked in torment, with wounds that none could see, and that none knew, except the Rogue and herself.

Yet there was never a word of complaint, and she loved her man through it all, standing by him always, because that is the way women go on. Thirty years she stood by him, hated and feared on the road the same as her husband, but never harmed except by the Rogue himself. And the pride of her eyes showed for her two strong sons, Dirk, now twenty-nine, and Nathan, twenty-eight.

There was little clan-closeness for the Enderley tribe any-where. When they pulled in at a wagon-meet there was no say for them, only men watching warily for the villain-trickery that always came, or women glancing pity and hatred together at Livvea, or young girls looking away when Dirk or Nathan met their eyes.

Now, of course, this would not be so good for Dirk and Nathan, both of them clean, hard, powerful young men, far more of the Calleran-kye than resembling Rogue Enderley. But what good was it for anyone to know that? Enderley-kye they were, and Enderley-kye they would remain, riding the North Wales Road with the Rogue their father, hated and feared because of the name they carried.

Dirk was the first to give a say about it. He gave a say one night outside Welshpool, on the old Roman road.

He said that neither he nor Nathan could take a mort to marry into the Enderley wagons, because all the road hated and feared them and no girl would come. Yet their only share of a wagon was here, with the Enderley-kye.

How must they wait for years without taking a mort? Or how must they go away, after their near-thirty years of work and willingness—go away without one coin or one wheel or one foal, to beg into some other wagon-clan?

Let Boar their father give them a wagon between them, which was little enough. Or let him give them the price of their two shares, and they would go away, to find morts for themselves, and then the Enderley-kye would still be on the road.

That was Dirk's say, clean and straight as the cut of a whip, like all his saying. But Rogue Enderley only turned him the cold little smile, and said he would see by next wagon-meet.

By next wagon-meet there was a sad story for the gorgia newspapers to print. A young gipsy-man had been ferreting for rabbits in an old sand-pit. Twenty feet of a sandbank had caved in, and it took the police nearly half a day to dig out Dirk Enderley's corpse. The kindly Welsh jury sympathized with the mother, as they gave their verdict of accidental death.

Then there was fear in Nathan's eyes. And horror in Livvea's. And in the eyes of the wagon-men of North Wales there was worse than fear and horror. For not even the vulture or jackal will eat its own young.

After that the travelling-people left the Rogue to himself, letting him have the best of the tatting-pitches and his choice of the camp-grounds. Wherever the wagons of the Enderley-kye pulled in, then the other wagons were harnessed at once, even if it was a winter midnight.

For now it was like a cancer-sore, and men waited for the Enderley tribe to die out, Livvea and Nathan and the Rogue, so that some time, maybe in years, the road would be clean again.

But in Nature the wheels go round the same as in a wagon, to make the flowers bloom and the fillies foal and the young men reach out for the young women. The wheels went round for Nathan Enderley, only there was nothing for him to do, except to go away, to Ireland or Scotland somewhere, penniless at thirty, to beg into the wagons of who would have him.

Only that remained. So it came the night that he made up his mind, and told his mother, and said good-bye, for he would go next day and never see Enderley wagons again.

And he never did.

At the Welsh end of Watling Street is a narrow, busy railway bridge, where the loaded motor-lorries go tearing by all night. A safe enough place for one on a motor-lorry, or one in a gorgia motor-car, but death for a careless man in a horse-wagon. One of the Enderley wagons went under a lorry at that bridge, before the next midnight—and from the wreckage there was none could point out proof whether Nathan had been locked in that wagon or not.

But every one on the road knew he had been locked in, knew that the Rogue had backed the wagon into danger. Livvea knew, too. Also she knew that because of that knowledge the Rogue would murder her as well.

For it was the end of her love and her patience, the end of her standing by the Rogue, and Livvea was going to the police. She would tell what she knew, and have the Rogue hung, not for his lifetime of villainy but for her murdered son Nathan alone.

Only, of course, the cold, cunning eyes of Rogue Enderley read all or nearly all that was in her mind, and Livvea knew that she too would be accidentally killed, soon, and before she had seen the police, if the Rogue could contrive it. So on the camp-common below Chester she walked to a wagon of the Cannadine, to people who had not spoken with her kye for years.

"I want no favour," she said, in a dull voice, to Josia Cannadine. "I want none, and I will ask none. But I will give a say, and you can listen if you wish."

"Give your say, Enderley Livvea," said the Cannadine woman, without warmth or interest. "Even the birds may listen to a say, and I am listening."

"My Nathan-son is dead below Llangollen," said Livvea. "Murdered by the Rogue, like so many another down the years. Now to-morrow I go to the plastramengros in Chester, and have the Rogue hung. He will kill me when he knows I have told," she went on, quietly as if she said it would rain, "and then that will be an end of the Enderleys, for he will hang at last."

There was silence by the Cannadine fire. No face showed friendliness, but there was pity on many, and sorrow for the woman whose life had been ruined and her sons destroyed. The Cannadine-kye waited.

"He will kill me when he knows," Livvea repeated dully, "and I care nothing. But if he will try," she hurried on, and her voice came up to a scream, "if he will try to have me killed to-night, by one of his accidents, so that I cannot tell the plastramengros, then this is my say. Some one of the Cannadine must go to Chester, to the plastramengros, and give the say I have given here. Now I will go back to my wagon.'

She turned away without another word, without waiting to hear whether the Cannadine would do as she asked, and she left troubled faces in the camp behind her. For of course no Cannadine, or any wagon-man, would think to carry stories to the housemen's police. In the first place, the police would not believe them, and would not understand if they did believe, so the result would only be trouble for all—except the Rogue.

Yet they could not sit and wait, well knowing that Livvea's words were only too true. The Rogue would read her eyes, would know what she intended—and there would be another sad accident before she got to the police. But what could the Cannadine do?

If Simon or one of the men killed the Rogue, in clean fight or by a gun-shot, then Simon and maybe more would be hanged, even if the gorgia believed about the Rogue, which they would not. Nor would it be of any help to give him a say, or to threaten him. For that would bring the slash in the

I

dark, the sly knife-cut, the poisoned rabbit, or some one other of the Rogue's tricks. That and nothing else.

The Cannadine men and women looked after Livvea as she went back to her wagon and to the Rogue. But they could not make their mind, or think of any way to have the thing finished.

Every one in the camp stayed awake that night. They waited for what they knew would come, although they did not know what form it would take—except that the Rogue would be proved innocent. It came sure enough.

By midnight in the blackness there were screams from the Enderley wagon, with a howling of dogs and the shouts of a man for help. Then in the darkness a burst of flames came up, and the Enderley wagon was on fire, with Livvea screaming inside and her husband outside fighting like mad to break down the door and save her.

The Cannadine rushed to help, with horse-buckets and axes, and Rogue Enderley wrought among them, working harder than any, but all to no purpose. Innocent Rogue Enderley, striving to save his wife from the burning wagon— there he was, and the Cannadine decided at last to tell the police.

But there was no need. The police arrived even before the wagon was burnt out, and Livvea's dead body was brought from the wreckage, while her husband sobbed wildly and the gorgia police looked on in sorrow and the Cannadine muttered in helpless hatred.

Then the police doctor found that Livvea's throat was cut, with the Rogue's razor, and the police found paraffin on the Rogue's trousers, and a can of paraffin had been upset in the wagon, with the wagon door locked and the key on the ground outside.

There was little need for much evidence at the trial, and no need for any of the wagon-people to give a say. Some news-writer among the housemen brought up the long list of accidents that was the Rogue's life-history. That would have been almost enough, without the razor and the paraffin and the key, and that was the end of Rogue Enderley.

To this day down the North Wales Road, men spit when his name comes up in a say. Then they laugh the hard laughter of the road and curse his name, until one of the Cannadine tells the story that only Josia Cannadine knew.

Love turned to hatred, mother-love deprived and turned into loathing, murder-fear turned into desperate and fearless suicide—that was the story. For Livvca had beaten the Rogue after all, and had done the thing herself before the Rogue could get at her.

Sure and double-sure she had made, that her death should look like murder contrived as an accident, and down the road men laugh again to think that the Rogue was innocent but once in his life—the time he was hanged.

CHAPTER TWELVE

The Say of the Syety

IT is my fixed intention to leave the road and go to live in north Buckinghamshire, some time soon after I am eighty. Many travelling-people keep the road long and long after that age, but they are real wagon-folk. Eighty will be old enough for me to go and settle down in north Bucks and write a few books. That is, of course, if I am not knocked down by a bus or atomized.

In the ordinary way I expect to live a long time, because I have spent many years on the road, and road-folk tend to stay alive for longer spells than townsfolk. My mother was ninety-five when she died (of an accident), but her family name was Colin and she had real wagon-wheels behind her. Ma Mella Scampe was a hundred and three the last time I saw her—helping to haul a bogged wagon out of a ditch on the Colchester Road. And among the travelling clans of Scotland there are *really* old folk.

A famous American doctor told the Pressmen of the United States that the three greatest enemies of civilized people, the three chief menaces to physical and mental health, were the alarm-clock, the telephone, and the calendar. Those who live on the road know none of the three, and that may be one reason they live so long. But, naturally, there are other factors as well, such as the healthy open-air life and the judicious mixture of hard work and laziness.

But one thing is certain. Wagon-folk live a long time. People in cities are generally unaware of this fact, and from this comes the Say of the Syety.

The first time I heard that say I guffawed out loud, and was only forgiven because the people thought I was drunk. There is no other say quite like it in the whole world.

It turns on the fact that travelling-people are few, poor, unimportant, secretive, and—unrecorded. Any intelligent office-man, filling in forms about the millions of people in the United States or Great Britain, will take little notice of the records about a few thousand putatively mendicant horse-drawn vagrants. That is, if there *are* any records, and there will not be many. Wherefore the wagon-folk do not figure much in city statistics.

The compilation of statistics has come almost to be a fine art in the last generation or so. A statistician can tell you how many people will be killed in motor accidents on Broadway or in Piccadilly the year after next. He can tell you an election result three months before the election. Without any trouble he can furnish the number of girls who will become typists this year, or the number of men between forty and fifty who will die during the next six months.

The research experts of insurance companies can even give the expectation of life for a person of any given age in any given occupation. By and large, they will be right, too. Just as the statisticians will be right about the number of accidents, or the incidence of *dementia præcox* among maiden ladies of sixty and over.

It is easy for uninformed people to laugh at the bureaucrats and the statisticians, but it is a fact that they really can forecast the ills and pleasures, the lives and deaths, of the populace-millions. The insurance companies alone venture a thousand million pounds a year on the correctness of the statistics, and they do not lose.

Unfortunately, a statistician would not look for—and would not get—any great body of information from the people who live in wagons. In any case, they are few. So they are counted in as being the same as other and normal folk—*i.e.*, city-dwellers. That is where the Say of the Syety comes in.

I had gone by Kirkley Run outside Lowestoft, to show my young son to an ancient woman of the Lambs. The boy was a good colt, and the Lamb-granny praised him. With eighty-odd years of experience among children—that is, eighty-odd years since she herself was first married—she liked the look of this boy, and liked his chances.

"A hundred he'll live," she announced. "Maybe *two* hundred. You'll give him the Syety, Jem?"

There were three of us near-strangers in the camp, and one looked at another for a clue, but none of us quite understood. So I said nothing. Whereupon old Leesa Lamb thought I was ignoring her advice, or was being careless about giving the Syety to the boy who would live to be a hundred or two.

"Every long-back boy should have the Syety," the old woman announced, dogmatically as if she spoke of vaccination or the care of a child's teeth. "You think what it is that a boy can start life, at fifty-five, with gold and silver money for ever and ever, if his kye but give him the Syety in time."

Censoriously she prosed on, plainly deploring the ignorance of some few old-fashioned thinkers who were not possessed of the new knowledge or by some bad luck had missed the great Say.

To make up for the harm the gorgia did years ago, she explained. To make up for the wrongs and the flogging and hanging of days gone by, the gorgia played fair in the end, and gave the good say. But even then it was nearly being missed, for some on the road—aye, most on the road—thought it was but more foolery of the housemen's papers.

But anyone will know that the housemen's papers are always fair and good—for the wagon-folk that will be. But when this gorgio came first, back at the time when they were fighting in the South African War, of course all on the road thought he was a twister, or mad. For this was his say.

"If you will give me one penny coin," says the gorgia to Sam Scampe, "and make an X on this paper, then we will have a good dicker." This is what he said. So of course Sam asked what was the dicker.

Now, the gorgio says that Sam was to give him one penny when he called each day (and where was he to call, with Sam out on the road, ranging far and fast) and Sam was to make an X on the paper. Now the Scampe boys laughed, and Ma Mella laughed, for it is not much of a dicker to say a man is to give you a brown coin every morning.

But, says the gorgio, if you die before you are seventy, then I will give Ma Mella the price of three horses, or maybe four horses it could be, if the horse-trade was poor at the time. If you die before you are seventy, says the gorgio.

He barely got out of the camp without being gelded, and Sam flaming mad shouting out that the gorgio was putting a nant on him, giving him bad luck, and wanting him to die for one copper coin. Then Ma Mella started to sob and scream, shouting out that she would not wish Sam dead for thirty horses, let alone three, and Sam reached out for the hazel cosh to mend the gorgio's manners.

But they fixed in the end that he meant no harm, but was just a twister like a three-card man, wanting a penny and pretending he wanted you to die, but not really wishing you dead at all, only desiring to take away the penny each week, or whenever you would give him one. So they let him go, and that was the end of the Syety say.

For a long time. But it came on one year that we were camped below Gorleston outside Yarmouth, after the races, and we were pulled in for three or four days to mend the harness and let a mare foal. And a Syety gorgio came to the camp again.

Now, it seemed that at this time, back forty-odd years, the Syety men were whipping up business everywhere they could, and the dead-penny, as Ma Mella called it, was spreading all over every town and city. But not among the wagon-folk, of course.

By thousand and million the townsfolk went in for the dicker about the dead-penny. A woeful thing, and a sad thing, but you know the strange ways people will act in a town. You think of a gorgia mother, with a chavo that is pride in her eyes, and she puts him in the dead-penny and makes her mark on the paper, and gives the penny each week, to get the gold money if that boy dies before he is forty, but if he does not die then the Syety gorgia keeps all the pennies.

You think of that mother's feelings—for the gorgia must have feelings too, somewhere—when that boy comes on to be thirty-nine, and she gives her say to herself. Now this will be her say—if only that son will die before his next birthday, then the gold money will come. But if he lives past forty then it is wagon-wreck and ford-flood, because the paper-man will keep all the pennies.

You think of that gorgia mother. But they did it. In millions, it was said. Only not wagon-folk, of course.

So—into the camp by Gorleston marched this gorgio, with his satchel of little printed papers, and his pens and pencils, and his kushti dollcie clothes. In he marched, and started to make his dicker about the dead-penny.

He hadn't got out twenty words before Lillamere Lamb reached down for the cosh, and Sam Scampe gave a growl, and jumped up with a harness-chain handy. So the gorgio near fainted with fear, and just in time he shouted out that he meant no harm. Just in time he gave out that the say was not about death, but about life.

Sam still watched him, warily enough, and kept hold of

the trace-chain. He waved the gorgio to sit down by the fire.

"Give your say," ordered Sam. "Only if there's one word about the dead-penny, or about me being made dead for three horses, you're done. Pull ahead."

"This is not about d-death," hurried the gorgio. "Quite the opposite. The opposite, gentlemen. It is about life." He breathed a bit more easily when Sam sat down.

"Will you dicker your three horses against a penny that my mort doesn't have a chavo by nine moon?" grinned Lillamere Lamb. "Is it that kind of life you mean, brother?" The gorgio worked up a sick sort of a smile, keeping one eye on the cosh by Lillamere's hand.

"In a way, sir," he said politely. "In—in a way." Then he glanced at some of his printed papers, and felt better, you could see, and drew a long breath.

"Compilation arrangement calculate adjustable," he said. "Average convertibility total benefit contribution accumulate. Capitalizate annuity foreclosable interchange."

Leesa glanced round the camp proudly, and watched for the nods of agreement from her hearers. Also she seemed to draw pleasure from the stupefaction on my own face.

"That was his say," she announced, in a complacent tone. "Do I not know it these forty-odd years? Like many another, I know it. Compilation arrangement calculate adjustable average convertibility total benefit contribution accumulate capitalizate annuity foreclosable interchange. That was his say."

She droned out the polysyllables, in a dry tone and all in perfect seriousness, plainly without the faintest notion what any single word meant. Her delivery was precisely that of a good character-actor depicting The Gentleman from the Prudential. I guffawed suddenly.

Old Leesa glared and frowned. Then she leant slightly towards me and relaxed.

"That rum with the bitter beer, Jem," she said jovially,

"below at the Fighting Cocks, is gone to your head. But pull your reins now and have the rest of the say like a good boy." I subsided.

"There was some word about spears," helped one of the women by the fireside. "Spears or shears."

"Later that came," snapped old Leesa. "Arrears. That came later. But that first day every one looked at the gorgia man, giving the lovely long-word say, until Sam Scampe tunnelled five words of sense out of him. He meant that you should dicker to stay alive, not die, and this was very different from the dead-penny."

"Now, do you mean, brother," said Sam slowly, "that if I give you a penny and make an X, then to-morrow if I am alive you give the price of the three horses?"

"No, no," cut in the gorgio, hurrying. "Not to-morrow, sir. But at a given age. What age are you, sir?" he asked Sam very brisk.

"Why?" said Sam.

So that looked the end of the life-penny say too. But Durkin Dunnaha from Cornwall, who had been over with horses to Beccles Fair, cut in and said the gorgio meant no harm, and to tell him some age, any age, for the sake of the say. Then Sam told he was forty.

The gorgio grabbed at once for his sheaf of printed papers and thumbed them over, and muttered bits of the say about convertibility and the like. Then at last he looked up and drew another long breath, to tell Sam that, if he gave one penny each day and made an X, then he would get fifteen guineas in hard money when he was fifty.

Sam thought a bit, and tried to count, although, of course, he could not reckon big counting like that. Then one of the chavos stepped in and whispered. So in the end Sam said it was not much of a dicker, not worth waiting ten years to make maybe ten shillings, when you could get ten shillings on the road in half a day. So the gorgio looked disappointed again.

"Wait a bit," put in Tildy—that's the youngest daughter of mine. "Wait a bit, and maybe we dicker after all. Because I may be fifty next week, or in a few days, anyway, according to the housemen's birth-papers. Now then—now then, I'll give you a penny and chance it, and make an X, and you give me the fifteen guineas next Thursday, if that's the dicker you want."

So we all crowded round to see had the gorgio the courage to take her at her word. But not he. Into the sheaf of papers he stuck his nose, muttering convertibilities again, and it seemed he would want a wicked lot of money from Tildy before he would give her fifteen guineas when she was fifty, because she was forty-nine already.

We got him down to bedrock in the end. And it was a good say after all, far better than we thought. Because this is what it came to. You paid him the pennies or shillings according to your age, more if you were older and less if you were young. Then if you lived to be fifty or more you got the money each week for ever. Now that was a fair dicker.

Tildy spoke up and said she would pay him a shilling a week, and Sam Scampe said the hell but he would go a sixpence and make an X, and another boy chanced eightpence because it looked fair. One of the Gaskins chanced for half a crown each seven days, they having done well at the tatting that year, and the gorgia man went away with a smile on his face, and a whole satchel of sixpences and shillings, and a whole show of X marks on printed papers.

So it went, and it spread, until hardly a person on wagon-wheels but had the Syety, the life-penny instead of the dead-penny. Till it came round for the first one to be paid, Jidbell Scampe, old Mella's great-granddaughter. A pound a week for ever she was to get, and we went into Norwich to see was the gorgio as good as his word.

Five wagons we had with us when we pulled into the centre of the city where the office was, and three flat drays with the chavos on, and a couple of loose colts that Jidbell's husband had picked up in Bungay on the way over. So we pulled up outside the office and went in, Jidbell first, clinging tight to her paper, and her husband behind with a small cosh, and Sam Scampe with a foot of lead pipe up his sleeve in case the gorgia man was a twister after all. And Ma Mella with her fingernails ready, and me.

The man at the desk was polite like we were gorgia ryes and rawnies, and gave chairs, and Jidbell showed her paper with the X on. So the man looked in a big book, and muttered bits about premium convertibility and the like, so we knew it was all right. Then he handed Jidbell a new pound note.

"And I'm to come every week?" asked Jidbell, cheeky, but only pretending because she wasn't really sure of it.

"Every week, madam," said the office gorgio. "But we can post it if you leave an address." And he looked out the window, to where the police had half the traffic of Norwich tangled up with the five wagons and the flat drays. "We can post it."

So they did, too. Week after week her money came, as reliable as the wind and rain. Then another paper became due, and another, and another. Until presently all the Scampikye, and all the Lamikye, and many another on the roads, had their good money coming from the gorgia man. All for paying the few coppers and making the X.

We never found out why he did it. Durkin Dunnaha gave a say that the gorgia man wasn't generous at all, but reckoned he would only have to pay out a bit, not much, and anyway less than you paid in. Because you were supposed to die soon after you were fifty. On account of the housemen die like that in the towns.

But that seems a poor say. For surely a gorgia man who knew long words like convertibility would know that people don't die that way. Forty-three years I draw my two pounds from the Syety, and thirty-nine years Ma Mella takes her three, and surely the gorgia would never expect to make money on *that* dicker. Especially with many another like us, up and down the country, travelling the road.

My own say is this, that the man meant well. From the start he said it was a reward for thrift and prudence, and he was a good man. Long years ago the gorgia did wrong things, flogging and hanging the people on the road for their thrift and prudence. Now they give the Syety, to make up for all, and good luck to them.

But the best of all is to come, Jem. For the best of all is on account of the chavos. For but one copper coin each day, or even each week, that chavo can buy his own kushti vado and his kushti gry, buy the best wagon and horse on the road, as soon as he comes to be fifty-five. In the towns a man might be thinking of dying, but on the road a boy can start off with the money from the Syety and live a hundred, with gold money coming in each week, coming until he gets maybe eighty times as much as his father paid in. For thrift and prudence, and because the gorgia want to be fair after all.

Leesa drew a long breath, and looked from my boy to myself. She ran her eyes over us both, measuring our physique, and I nearly guffawed again as I thought that an insurance doctor was supposed to do the same thing—but in reverse.

"You'll give the colt the Syety, Jem," she insisted. "For, even if you be house yourself, he's Colin-kye anyway, and a long-back. A hundred he'll make—and you think how glad the gorgia will be to pay him for his thrift and prudence, the same as they pay us, these two score years and only started."

Plainly the truth about the Say of the Syety was with Dunnaha from Cornwall. The statisticians did not know that romani people live a long time, that was all.

In the compilation of statistics re longevity, on an actuarial basis the extremely diminutive nomad populace would not in any marked degree diminish the rate of computable interest concomitatant with the normal coefficient of survival, and urban-populace benefits would still be applicable.

Or, in other words, it is a fair dicker.

CHAPTER THIRTEEN

Boricosh Kuka Drom

SNAKES are uncommon in England and Scotland, but the word occurs often in the speech of the wagon-people of both countries. A word like 'sap,' which is the romani term for a snake, will crop up in a hundred forms, thinly disguised, as in 'springo,' which means a snake-charmer.

This leads some historians to believe that the romani people came originally from India or somewhere near it. Which seems fair enough. Others will say that in the distant past their ancestors must have been snake-worshippers. Which is fair enough, too.

Besides this, at least one scholar has made out a very good case for claiming that the original progenitors of all the romani were a crowd of non-Jewish people who cleared out from Egypt at the time when the Jews were going. These people went with the Jews out into the desert, but started a mutiny when times got bad.

At the time when, according to the Old Testament, the Jews were being fed on manna, the crowd of non-Jews protested, remembered the good food they had left behind in

Egypt, and apparently cleared out again. Although it seems possible that some of them, at least, stayed behind, and set up the golden-serpent worship, or helped to set it up.

But along that particular scholarship road there are pitfalls innumerable. It is one thing to find that a people are fond of using the word 'sap' (which is only 'serp' anyway, the old form of serpent). To wish a background of snake-worship on them because they like talking about saps is quite another matter. But it is exactly the kind of thing any decent, well-intentioned scholar would do—if all his information came from people who could neither read nor write, and who regarded him as a halfwit into the bargain!

The trouble—and it is a pleasant and kindly thing rather than otherwise—arises because people in towns will insist, naturally enough, on regarding the wagon-folk as romantic and strange and different. Of course, the notion is well based; they *are* strange: a person needs only one look at them to know that much. But the town-man, and especially the scholar, wants to be told about the romance and the strangeness all the time. He will ask questions about the worship of the Golden Calf, or about the philological significance of Oriental terminology—ask them of some poor wagon-woman hurrying to the grocer's, and wondering if the butter-ration will be increased this week.

Is it any wonder that the scholars are told lies from one end of England to the other?

There is another aspect of the matter. House-folk, both men and women, are by and large generous to the wagon-people. They pity the nomads because they have no homes, and they very often transmute the pity into a sixpence or a shilling. It is a good thought and a kindly, like giving a few crumbs to a robin because he has no loaf and you have. True, he may have a whole gardenful of worms, and you may know it, but the fact does remain that *you* have a loaf. So the robin gets the crumbs.

Thus it comes that the rôle of homeless wanderer is

practically forced on the wagon-folk, especially the women. If they are young women and pretty, or very old women of powerful personality, the homeless wandering is all the more romantic for that.

Somewhere in another book, about tramps, I pointed out that the professional tramp's chief stock-in-trade was the horizon, the far-away place from which he is supposed to have come or to which he is supposed to be going. That far-away factor is even more powerful when a street-person talks with a wagon-person.

Here is the wagon, and here is the horse. Here is the sunburn of many days on the women and children. Here too are the dropped words about horse-markets far distant, the curious-looking clothes and tools and furniture. It is far Cathay and Samarkand come to the city housewife's door, or come to meet her when she strolls in the country, and she rewards it accordingly.

But it so happens that she nearly always asks the same stock questions. So that the wagon-people come to know the answers that are expected of them, tend to hurry the responses out like a careless priest gabbling a litany, and get on along the road—about their business, or as far as the next person who wants to ask romantic questions for sixpence.

Nevertheless, it is a fair dicker. And both sides know it. People who live in towns are squeezed fairly tightly together, in mind and body, for most of the time. It does them good to know about non-city life, about the wild, and to meet it face to face. It does them far more good than reading books or seeing films.

So that the romani woman is really a show-person, just as much as a theatrical producer. The city woman has need of a glimpse at the road. The wagon-woman has need of a sixpence. It is a fair dicker.

Precisely the same thing is true in the case of the tramps. Except that the wagon-people do not bother to invent stories, sticking to the simple facts of their wild life, while the tramp

rings the changes continually and produces new stories to fit
new needs.

Perhaps the tramps have to. Because *their* origins are not
shrouded in mystery! The romani people tell little or nothing.
But townsfolk continually ask, especially scholars. It is a good
thing, but sad in a way, because none of the scholars get any
chance to come by information.

After all, you simply can *not* walk up to a strange man and
offer him half a crown to tell you whether his grandfather was
hanged or not. Unless he lives on wagon-wheels, when for
some reason most people think you can.

Earlier in this book I referred to my own chance of asking
intimate questions by a Cannadine fire. The comparison I
made is exact. One must really imagine Sam Scampe walking
into a bank and, instead of doing any business, commencing to
ask questions about the bank-manager's wife's father.

Thus the 'tale' has become one of the lesser tools of the
wagon way of life. So many clothes-pegs, so much tatting,
so much horse-trading, so much basket-work, so much 'tale'
—if a wagon-family counted their sources of income the list
might come something after that fashion.

Which is satisfactory to every one concerned, giver and
receiver alike. Except for the kindliest people of all, the most
sympathetic and most generous—the scholars. *They* make
themselves a nuisance continually, meaning well all the time.
The gabbled stock-responses mean nothing to them, and they
seek always for the truth behind. Often from people in whose
language there is no word for truth! Sometimes the results
are amusing.

I am reminded of Hacky Packer, from Long Melford.
Hacky used to do a bit of tatting, then made out well, and has
a store now, where he buys the tat from others on the road.
He does a good deal of horse-trading, buys and sells furniture,
attends auctions and sales all over Norfolk and Suffolk. One
day he was stopped by a man on the road from Long Melford
to Lavenham.

K

"A good little gorgia man," Hacky reported. "With nice little gold-rimmed eye-glasses—worth nine quid, I'd have said —and a suit of Scots tweed on him that was as rum-looking as my own whipcords. But the whipcords cost me twenty-six quid in Norwich, and this little man's battered tweed suit ran him a lot more. A good dollcie mush, with pens and pencils on him, and a peering way through the glasses, and you could *feel* he was a good fellow down inside.

"'Good-bye, Father,' he says in romani, and I guess that he means to say 'Good morning, brother,' so I says hello. Then he asks where I'm going!

"Now, anyone outside the madhouse knows you shouldn't say a thing like that. But the little fellow looked so good and smelt so decent that I told him quiet enough. Being bound for Lavenham, I said I was going to London. He takes out two half-crowns.

"'Are you married?' he asks, and I tell him yes. He hands me one of the half-crowns.

"'Twice I've been married, sir,' I tells him at once, natural enough, but he sticks to the second tosharoon, and writes a few words in a little book. Then he takes out another tosharoon, and holds the two half-crowns together in front of me.

"'Tell me,' he says. 'Did you drink your wife's urine as part of your marriage ceremony?'

"Now I was in a hurry to Lavenham, and had a little hangover besides, after a big horse-dicker the night before. But instead of driving the horse over him I waited. Because he *was* a nice little gorgio inside him. So I started to whistle *I love my Wife, I love Her Dearly*, same as we used to sing in France in the 'Fourteen War. But he's too slow to get that. So I told him that all I drank was a pint and a half of whisky at the Black Boy in Sudbury, and that I was married by a parson the same as himself.

"Well, he was bitterly disappointed. That came out like a rock on the road. Bitterly disappointed—so, of course, I was sorry. And as soon as he asked me if I liked hedgehog I said yes, we had it every day. Then he asked me who cooked it, and how, and I had to make up a say about my wife wouldn't let anyone cook the hedgehog but herself, and good-bye now because I was in a hurry to Lavenham, not London. But it was no use.

"'Does your wife tell fortunes?' he asked next, and I said there was none better on the road. That was a fair enough say, me being without a wife at the time. Then he gave me the two half-crowns, and you could see how proud he was, to be giving me seven-and-six. But at the same time you could see he was heartbroken about my not having drunk my wife's piss, and got back to it again and again.

"'You are telling me the truth?' he says, and I nearly said no—he looked so pitiful. If only I'd known in time, for he was a decent little fellow, and the good gold-rimmed glasses on him, and the top-tree Scots tweeds—if only I'd known in time. Here—if you know *I love my Wife, I love Her Dearly* then you know the bit that goes before the wooden spoon. If only I'd known he was going to take it so bad I'd have told him the wooden-spoon bit and made him happy. So I went on into Lavenham, and was half an hour late for the sale."

The Hacky story was funny enough. But there were other sides to it. Like many another, I know the song *I love my Wife*, one of the unprinted and unprintable songs beloved of the P.B.I. during the First World War. It is a great loss to scholarship that Hacky did not give the earnest inquirer the "wooden-spoon bit," to save him from disappointment.

The other side of the story is that Hacky probably lost eighteen or twenty pounds by being late for the auction. As he knew he would, even while he was humouring the earnest inquirer because he smelt good. All the kindliness and generosity were not on the seven-and-sixpenny side that morning.

That kind of 'research' has been going on among the romani people for centuries. Small wonder that weird and contradictory assertions have crept into the books. Not even a Sussex farm-labourer will answer intimate questions about his family life to a perfect stranger.

So it is possible that the sap story, the ancient background of serpent-worship, may have started from a more or less jocular falsehood from some wagon-man like Hacky Packer in the past. Of course, it may be all true—I myself am prepared to believe even stranger things about my road-friends.

But anyone who has read this book as far as here will know that the wagon-people, even more than the tramps, have good cause for the use of deception against all and sundry who ask prying questions.

What sensible person would believe a tramp's account of himself? How, then, is one to take an illiterate wagon-man's account of his great-great-grandfather's private life?

The answer is that no direct question is of the slightest use. Indeed, it is much more likely to do harm. To the inquirer, that is, if he be a gorgia, and especially if he is an official.

Wherefore I lay by a fire one evening, and warmed myself, and preened myself, while a man asked questions. He asked the questions of Black Harry Smith and his family. I preened myself because, although I was a houseman and almost a stranger, I had sufficient good sense to lie there and say nothing. The visitor asked questions.

Also I was secretly amused, as were Josia Smith and her husband, because the stranger took me for one of the family. (Little did he know that I was only tolerated, and given a tin of tea, because my mother's family name was Colin and because I had been in gaol with Charlie Baker!)

It is not a very good foundation for intimacy, that. Nor for scholarship founded upon intimacy. Yet it is the only one, as I soon knew when the visitor got down to business.

This was no fool, to say "Good-bye, Father" in the romani language when he intended to say "Good morning, sir." Neither was he a sentimentalist, expecting Black Harry to play a guitar and sing Spanish songs—Black Harry never having been far from Hertfordshire in his life. This was a scholar, who knew what he wanted, and set about getting it.

A writer of detective stories in search of copy who visited

a thieves' pub and asked the habitués for details about their jobs would have had about the same chance. It was a pity, for the man liked the romani people, and he was after the serpent-worship story.

He nearly had it, too, and I could see the quest-glint in his eyes as he looked round the camp. This was on the long grass slope above Whipsnade, outside the fence of the Zoo. (There is always a rake of romani wagons there. Rabbits and other valuable vermin multiply vastly inside that fence—but that is another story.)

The two Smith wagons, with a flat dray and two four-wheeled trolleys, were backed into a curve on the ancient turf. Almost certainly there had been a Britons' camp there in an earlier day, and a Roman camp later, and maybe a last forlorn-hope camp of the East Anglians later still.

Josia Smith and her sister haunch-squatted by the fire and watched the stranger's face. Black Harry and I lay side by side, Harry answering questions, I grinning stupidly when addressed, because the man would have spotted me for a foreigner the moment I spoke.

Twenty yards away the children played, round a wooden erection like a tall cross. They danced round the cross-piece, as children dance round a maypole, singing, first one and then another darting in to fix a flower in place.

The cross was about six feet high, with the cross-piece very near the top, and the children had twined a long strand of ivy from side to side. They sang as they danced, each one carrying a bunch of wild flowers, and at every pause in the song there was a pause in the dancing. Then the boy or girl whose turn it was darted in and tried to fix his or her flower on the long, snaking garland in one swift dab before jumping back into line.

Like all wagon-children's play, it was part and parcel of their work. If a flower was placed correctly there was a shout of "Boarie, boarie." If it fell there were jeers, a shouting of "Drum," and the circling dance recommenced.

The song had only about twenty lines, and was repeated again and again, with an often-recurring phrase for punctuation, about a boricosh kuka the drom. I had seen the game before, with nearly similar words, up in Scotland, and paid little attention except to note that the visitor seemed to know it too.

He glanced at the youngsters from time to time, while he quarried patiently for non-evasive answers from Black Harry. He wanted to know if Black Harry believed in God.

Harry's reply was roughly to the effect that he meant to say, brother, of course every man believed in something, didn't he, that stood to reason, and he meant to say, as a matter of fact, well, and did the brother believe in God himself, now?

Which was not too good value for the five shillings Josia had been given to buy sweets for the children. But the caller was no fool, and plugged on patiently. Did Harry and Josia go to church?

When they could, was the perhaps inevitable answer. When they could, brother. But, of course, with people moving about, here and there, of course you never knew where you were, did you?

The visitor thought for a moment, running his eyes round the camp, glancing at the singing children, then at the innocent faces of Black Harry and his wife, then back to the children. It was clear that he knew the words of the song.

> Hurry down, lady proud,
> From thy castle-court fair
> To the bend where thy lover may come.
> To the golden-brown love with the ringlet black hair
> By the boricosh kuka the drom.

Sometimes, he told Harry, he went to church himself. It all depended what country he was in—sometimes a Catholic church in Ireland, and sometimes it was a mosque. Travelling-people knew how it was. And had Josia, or Harry, ever heard that years ago travelling-people used to worship a bull, perhaps of stone? There was silence.

Having been a professional tramp, I understood that silence. We call it looking for a lead. What, in other words, does the inquirer *want* to be told? It is important. Because on a correct choice may depend the tramp's shilling or florin or pound. Harry and Josia were looking for a lead. There would be more than the sweet-money to come.

Good luck to Black Harry, he found the right answer, precisely the answer I had fixed on myself, although he was not a professional tramp; and was no scholar.

In Cornwall, he stated frankly, there were all kinds of stone animals. And the wagon-people had been in Cornwall for a long time. And he meant to say, brother.

In a manner of speaking, he went on, as he felt his way and watched the visitor's face—in a manner of speaking you could put it that them stone animals wasn't put there for fun. No. Not of course that you could say the wagon-people put them there. But, to tell the truth, the wagon-people *had* been a long time in Cornwall.

It was the right lead. Josia sighed contentment. The inquirer breathed satisfaction. There was talk about stone bulls. But always in the talk the visitor kept one ear cocked for the song of the dancing children.

> Carry load from afar,
> Lonely wanderer, astray,
> Like the honey-bee far from his comb.
> Round the bend may be love, and a welcome to stay
> By the boricosh kuka the drom.

Skilful questioning led Black Harry, willingly enough, from stone bulls to stone fishes, and stone snakes, and iron snakes, and brass snakes. But by that time Harry Smith had the lead and knew the answers.

As the gentleman no doubt knew, he pointed out, all their family were smiths of one kind and another.

Some, he admitted modestly, some said their family had *started* the smith thing. Maybe not, but they had in fact been smiths a long time, maybe hundreds of years if a man knew the truth. Make anything out of iron or brass, anything. Uncle of his made steel flowers and copper snakes and brass birds for a pair of gates, the loveliest copper snakes a man could see. Aye. Copper snakes.

It wouldn't be fair, he indicated—it wouldn't be *fair* to put it that any wagon-man anywhere ever prayed to any snake. No. But it stood to reason, and a man had to admit it, that in a way them stone snakes and copper snakes and so on must be a kind of God for some one. Not for Black Harry, of course, but at the same time he meant to say.

So the talk went comfortably to snakes, and to the song the children were singing, and to questions as to why they sang it as they played round a cross with a long snake of ivy twined over it. Not once did the caller ask what the few strange words meant, and mentally I scored that omission to his credit. But he listened carefully as the children went on.

> Totter on, weary crone,
> Thou shalt slumber, and soon,
> When the reaper thou findest at home.
> At the end of thy quest
> By the bend thou shalt rest
> Nigh the boricosh kuka the drom.

He was a good man, a competent craftsman as an inquisitor, what we would call a slick interviewer in Fleet Street. I knew he had memorized the sounds of the three or four romani words, and would dig out their meaning somewhere before he was much older. Also I knew he had appraised at their true worth Harry's every awkward hesitation and attempt at evasion. He finished his questioning and went away satisfied.

Josia was satisfied, too. Black Harry was satisfied. So was I. Now, *that* was a successful interview, to please every one concerned.

But how could the poor devil know that gipsy children play at learning their work, just as kittens play at learning to catch mice? The circle-dance with bunches of flowers, performed as play, shows a profit later on when the children make posies and have to be nimble and skilful with their fingers.

He was on the right track about the song. It is an old song, about something that bulks largely in the lives of all travelling-people, whether wagon-folk or otherwise. For city people everything of importance happens in the home. For tramps and other homeless wanderers the place where things happen is at the cross-roads. The wooden cross had the transverse arm very near the top. I think the interviewer missed that.

Tober is the travelling-word for a road—that is, a highway. But for the road on which one walks the word is drom. Kuk is to look or glance. Kuka is looking or pointing. Cosh is timber, a pole, a post. Bori or burra is tall.

Boricosh kuka the drom. The tall pole pointing down the road. The song is about a signpost.

CHAPTER FOURTEEN

Boney Bosivel

IT is a story the mothers will tell the chavos at night, to keep them from straying. Straggling round the camp in the dark, a chavo might go over a rock-bank or into a briar brake, or trample on his father's nets and traps. At such a time the mothers frighten them back to the fires, telling them Boney Bosivel will get them.

One strange thing is that, although it is a big say, it does not carry the name of the man who started it all, but the name of the good man he drove to misery and death, a boy of the Bosivels out of Lincolnshire. The other fellow's name can be said, Liltie Hearn, and it may be that there was never one other man like him in the world.

Because Liltie is the only romani man you'll ever hear of—the only one—who forgot his people and his blood. Many another clan of people keep close, and stand by their own at need, the English and the Jews, the Sicily men and the Irish, so the thing is known and understood.

They say that you will be in a crowded lane in Shanghai, with Chinese by the hundred and thousand thick as wasps on a jam-pot, and if some one shouts for help in English then the nearest Englishman jumps in without asking one word. The Jews, too—for a thousand years people know how they stand by their own. Most of them, anyway. Plain say it is about the Irish, also; how a million-pound Irisher will be pals with a mumping tramp Irisher if they meet on a foreign road.

But of all those there are exceptions, and only among the romani people was there never an exception, down through how many hundred years no one can say. Never one, and every one knows it. That is why Liltie Hearn has no other man like him in the world; he was the only different one.

Liltie left the road and came rich, and forgot his own people, and hated his own people, and drove one of the best of the romani to hunger and slavery and death. For the price of one · horse and a tent, back in the time when they were fighting in the war at Waterloo.

It was long before then that Liltie got off the road to stay. Many another did at the time. A person could say the names, for they are all good names. In 1800 or then the first lot of romani people left the road, but none of them ever forgot. To this day. Except Liltie.

You could see the places they came by. By the edge of Newmarket Heath, where there are towns and villages now, many such a place started when a romani wagon pulled in and stayed. By Big Melford Common, in Suffolk, and Creek Common, in Norfolk, and Epping Forest, in Essex—in many a place there is a big house now, or even a village of big houses, and all from one romani man who left the road and settled down.

That was how Liltie Hearn did it. He left the road and pulled in his wagons, on a little patch of common land that no one cared about, by Woodbridge, near Ipswich. For the first year he lived in his wagon, and made no show of wanting anything from anyone, but had little patches of garden and a few vegetables, all the most natural thing in the world.

Then the next year he had a bit of a hut, but still kept the

wagons there. So that he looked like a romani man just pulled
in for a week or two. The patches of garden and vegetables
were bigger by that time, and a straggling scrap of a fence
here and there, but nothing that anyone would notice much,
for the common land was still fairly plenty in those days.

So it went on from year to year, with Liltie's fence spreading
fast and far, until in the end he had a big house, and a fence
round enough land to make him rich without anything else.
But there was plenty else, because Liltie was well in and made
money fast. Crooked or straight he made it.

And then one day suddenly he cut loose and had no more
to do with his own people, and denied them, and hated them.
Up to then, in the ordinary way, if a romani tribe came the
road north from Ipswich, and if they pulled in near Liltie's,
in the natural way they went over, and gave a say. Then if
they wanted anything they asked for it, or if Liltie wanted
anything they gave it, in the ordinary run of the road.

But when Liltie had the money, quite suddenly and with no
warning he cut adrift. And the first thing any road-folk knew
was that one night when a rake of the Scampe wagons pulled
in by Liltie's all the citizens (that was Liltie's men) and the
soldiers, and the watch (that was the plastramengros, because
the police wasn't invented yet in those days)—all the rake of
them swept in and fought the Scampes out of it. And go they
must, when they got over their surprise, because Liltie would
have handed them over to be transported to Botany Bay,
as was done with travelling-people in those days. They went,
and no romani wagon ever pulled in there again.

So Liltie prospered, and was rid of the thought that he came
from the road—except maybe at night when he would be
afraid of what he had done. There was a big war in Europe
at the time, in the days before the battle of Waterloo, and
Liltie made money fast, selling horses to the gorgia Government for the soldiers, or buying the metal to make the guns.

Some do that in every war, they say. Liltie came richer
still. There might be two hundred horses on his land, and his

land alone worth ten thousand pounds, and a bank of scrap-iron that was worth thousands more, for the Government in the Waterloo war.

Now it came on that Waterloo was fought, and the English gorgia won, and the war was over. Now in the peace after that war there were bad times on the road. Because the roads were full thick with men who had been in the soldiers and had nowhere to go.

Terrible laws were passed against them, naming them for sturdy vagrants, and giving them the style of rogues and vagabonds, and a man could be transported for life if he was a starving ex-soldier and stole four copper coins or a loaf. A strange reward for winning Waterloo, but it was always like that after a big war. Except not now, of course.

Now Liltie is sitting at home one night when his flunkey-man said there was a man named Bosivel had called. So Liltie had him in, he not having seen even one man from the road at close quarters for many a year.

The Bosivel boy came in, a boy who had been away for years, in the gorgia ships where he was put from the press-gang, and in the gorgia soldiers after that, and at the battle of Waterloo. So he knew nothing, not one word, of what Liltie had turned out in the years between, but expected to find friendship and help by Liltie's fire, as any romani would at need. He came in, and made a sign, and gave Liltie good luck in romani.

"Reuben Bosivel," he says all cheerfully. "The son of Big Nathan. And good luck, Liltie—long years I see none of our people, for I have been to the French war." He stands and smiles and waits for his welcome.

Sad man. Sad man. Waiting for a welcome from Yellow Liltie Hearn!

"What d'you want?" says Liltie, gruff and fierce as any plastramengro, and the Bosivel boy stared.

"From the trooper-ship below Ipswich I come," he explained, "and I must get to my people, by Lincoln. The roads are full thick with broken soldiers, and the plastramengros will gaol me to-morrow, before I make Woodbridge, if I have to beg my way."

"What d'you want?" snarled Liltie again.

"A horse if you have one," says the Bosivel boy. "And a tent if you have one. And a pair of pistols to make my road to Lincoln. With a trifle of hard money, if such you can spare. Then all will be well, and the next time our wagons pull in here the Bosivel-kye will square for all, and good luck, Liltie."

"Get on your road," says Hearn. "We want no thieving didicai here. Get on your road."

"Am I telling you," says Reuben Bosivel, "that on the road I shall not stay free six hours. There is no trial, as you know, and it means Botany Bay if I so much as snare one rabbit for my supper." And he stared again, for he could still not believe his ears, for never up to then had anyone heard of a romani man turning against his own.

"So be it for Botany Bay," says Yellow Liltie Hearn. "So be it and get out." Reuben Bosivel turned away.

"So be it, if it must," he said quietly. "Now I go the road into Woodbridge. But, Liltie," he puts in, still very quiet, "even from Botany Bay I shall come to thank you. Even if I die there, yellow one. They call me Bonaparte Bosivel in the soldiers, because I stick my word. Boney Bosivel, and I shall stick my word for you, whether I stand or fall to-morrow. Whether I stand or fall, and bad luck, Liltie, and remember."

He walked out, and within five miles of the house the plastramengros had him, for a stolen pheasant and a stolen loaf of bread. Maybe Liltie breathed good relief in a few weeks when he heard the news. For to Botany Bay the boy went sure enough.

There is no way of knowing what went on in Liltie Hearn's mind in the years that came. But in outside things he went prospering fast. A rich man he was, coming fifty-odd, when he heard the good news that a convict called Boney Bosivel had died far away over the sea.

So Liltie sat back and looked round to make more money, and throve and throve again. The richest man by Wood-bridge he was, and like to marry the high lord's daughter, so he would be happy, no doubt. Until one night, walking late through his estate, which was bigger than ever by then, a dark figure stepped out of a wood. Thin and ghastly he looked, only a skeleton, with a bony face that gave the cold-blood to Liltie Hearn, but he made no hostile move.

"Boney Bosivel," he said cheerfully. "The son of Big Nathan. And good luck, Liltie—long years I see none of our people."

"Keep back," shouted Liltie Hearn. "Keep back. Boney Bosivel is dead, in Botany Bay."

"Dead indeed," agreed the tall figure. "Dead I be, and come to remind you. Did I not promise to thank you, and they call me Boney Bosivel because I stick my word."

He moved a few inches closer to Liltie's horse, and Liltie screamed for help and fumbled for his pistols, then drew breath again as the horse dashed away, and the thin dark man made no move to follow him. Next day Hearn lay close, terrified, but presently he forgot, and before long he could believe, or nearly believe, he had made the say himself, out of a worried mind. In three weeks he was himself again, and then one night the skeleton-like man looked in at Liltie's bedroom window.

"Boney Bosivel," he said, in a cheerful voice. "The son of Big Nathan. Come to thank you, Liltie. You'll remember my promise."

Yellow Liltie Hearn nearly choked then and there. But when he screamed for help, and the servants came, there was no one at the window or near it. For three days Liltie refused to stir out of his bedroom, lying in bed with two pistols beside him, and shivering day and night.

But a business-man has business, and after a week Hearn was out and around again. There was no sign from Boney, but Liltie began to go thin, and did not sleep, and often he screamed when he thought he saw the thin black man who was not there at all. Then gradually he calmed, and was making to be healthy again, when the black one popped out one night from the side of the road by Woodbridge.

"Boney Bosivel," he said, cheerfully as ever. "To give you thanks, as was my promise. Boney Bosivel, and I stick my word for ever." Liltie Hearn did not hear the last word or two, for he was down on the road in an apoplexy, and was a sick man for a month.

Long before the month was over, and before Liltie was properly well again, he had a shock of another kind. For one day he tottered round his estate for exercise, and over on the common he saw a ring of wagons and tents, the ash-tam tents whose shape he knew of long time, the camp of the Bosivels.

He rallied after a minute, for a man who will steal half a common, and mass up thousands, and swear his own kin away, must have courage of a kind. He rallied, and with twelve armed men round him he went over that afternoon to the camp of the Bosivels, and shouted for their leader.

Big Nathan Bosivel was there, the father of Reuben who was dead, and Simon Bosivel, the young brother of Reuben, and Rachel Bosivel, who was the mother of the dead boy. They sat to look at Liltie Hearn, and gave him no say or salutation, made him no road-sign, but waited to hear his voice. He wasted no words.

"Call off your curs," he ordered. "Call off your curs and your corpses, for, dead or alive, I am afraid of no Bosivel. Call him off, I tell you, or I will blow your whole camp to thistledown by night."

The family looked at him in silence, and every one round by the fire turned him the same cold smile. No one spoke for a long time.

"Easy seen that you are not afraid," said Big Nathan at last. "Since you come to order us, the living, to speak for you with the dead. To speak with which one of our dead?" He smiled, and the mother smiled, and young Simon smiled in turn, while they watched Liltie Hearn and gloated over the fear that was behind his boasting.

"If Boney Bosivel comes near me again," said Hearn at last, "then the soldiers from Ipswich will blow every Bosivel here into bits off this common. I can do it, as you well know, and I *will* do it."

"And that," said Big Nathan quietly, "will stop Boney Bosivel from sticking his word, yes? Ah, no, Liltie, not a Bosivel. How long," he asked pleasantly, "how long was it my son said he would come to thank you?"

"For ever, he said," put in Simon Bosivel. "And for ever it will be if I know my dead brother. He sticks his word."

Then Hearn's nerve gave out, and his voice went quavering, and he begged with the old mother that he had meant no harm. He begged with her, because of course he had the dark-fear inside him still, being a wagon-man at bottom, and craved her to call off her dead son.

"Can I go to Botany Bay and whisper into his grave?" she asked him. "What am I, that I should put between a dead man and his word? If Reuben said for ever it is for ever. Good-bye."

Liltie made a peace sign as he left, but no one responded, and he tried to speak fair words, but the Bosivel-kye only smiled. Still Hearn spoke them well, and left the common and crossed on to his own estate.

Crossing a little bridge on his estate, by a high rock-bank where he could see the tents of the Bosivels, but was safe far within his own fence, he swore then and there that he would bring soldiers, with a grapeshot gun, and blow the rest of the Bosivels to hell with Boney, and he was not afraid of them dead or alive. But that was by daylight and in the midst of his armed servingmen. Still, he meant to do it, and made haste to his house, to send the messenger riding for Ipswich, when a carriage came driving to the door and a lady got out.

This was the daughter of the high lord of Woodbridge, one

L

with whom Liltie was hoping to wed. Fifty he was, and the wealthiest man for miles, so he could lay claim to the hand of the gorgia lady, a beauty and warm-hearted smiling one, sold him by her father, it was said, when by right she would marry with some one young like herself. From his upstairs window Liltie saw her come from her carriage, and went down the stairs to meet her.

He saw her pass through the hall, following a servant to the drawing-room, and hurried down to speak of marriage, forgetting his errand to have the Bosivels destroyed. He opened the door, and saw the tip of her shoe where she sat in a long chair by the fireside.

Then she stood up, and it was not the high lord's daughter, but a thin man, chalk-white and cold.

"Boney Bosivel," he said in the same cheerful tone. "To thank you and keep my word. For ever."

Liltie Hearn went down as if he had been poleaxed. When he came round there was no one in the room, and he squealed like a hare in a trap till the servingmen came.

He squealed still, with his armed men round him, while a messenger fetched a lawyer out of Woodbridge. And when the lawyer came Liltie made his will, leaving every penny he owned, and every acre he owned, to the Bosivel tribe for ever. Then, and then only, he slept.

Next day he felt happier than he had ever felt since the first night he saw Boney Bosivel, and he walked that afternoon to the Bosivel camp, to tell his news and make his peace. They received him well, and all was friendship again, and even the old mother gave her say that it was a noble thing to do, making up for the wrong.

So Liltie whistled for the first time in years, as he crossed the little bridge going back into his estate. His money was gone, but he did not mind, for his peace was made, and that was better than money. By the rock-bank he stood smiling, as he glanced back at the Bosivel tents, and at his elbow some one spoke from the trees.

"Boney Bosivel," said the thin dark man. "The son of Big Nathan. I stick my word. For ever."

Liltie Hearn went over the rock-bank, and was picked up with a broken neck.

That is the story the mothers will tell, to keep the chavos from straying off the camp-ground. All Liltie's house and lands came into the Bosivel family, and the first thing they did was to flatten Liltie's house until no stone was over another stone anywhere.

To this day there is nothing there, neither growing nor standing. Where the road comes by the place of Liltie's former home there is a grave by the roadside, an empty grave for the man who died in Botany Bay. To this day fresh flowers go on it, and the country people will tell you that "wandering gipsies," as they say, come far to lay them there.

And when the wagons pass the way each one is pulled aside for a moment by the rock-bank where Liltie Hearn went over, and the men make water on his grave while they curse his name. Then some one will give the say of Boney Bosivel.

But the way some tell it, all the work was done by young Simon, the thin brother of the dead man. Partly with the help of the lord's daughter, who, like many another high-born lady, was in love with a romani boy.

They say Simon frightened Liltie into giving away everything he owned to the Bosivels. Then frightened him at last until he fell over the bank.

And if he did—good luck to him.

Then others will tell that when Simon had Liltie scared, and all his lands were signed away, he got at Liltie before he had time to change his mind, and pushed him over the bank to make sure.

And if he did—good luck to him.

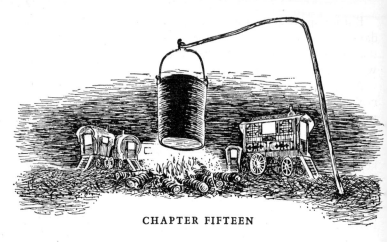

CHAPTER FIFTEEN

The Say of Colin Colin

VERY often those meeting an Australian for the first time, say an Australian soldier down Fleet Street, in London, will be surprised to find that he has an Irish-sounding name. Australia is an English colony, not an Irish.

Yet the Irish-sounding names will come up again and again, until a stranger might think there was no one at all in Australia but people from Tipperary or Mayo. Donal and Conal, Kelly and Duane, Delancy and Tuohy, Sullivan, Kieran, O'Connel, and Flaherty—they come thick and fast out of Australia, and out of New Zealand, too.

There is considerable amusement in this fact, especially when one talks with a person whose family have been long resident in Australia. Because, of course, Australian history does not go very far back.

English people boast sometimes that their families came over with William the Conqueror. Americans will say their people arrived in the *Mayflower*. Many an Irishman will claim that his family have lived in the same place for a thousand years. Every one knows the kind of thing.

But for an Australian who claims to trace back to the earliest days it is a hard choice. For how is he to decide—is he to boast that his ancestors were convicts? Or is he to claim that they were warders?

A few people in this country, and many in Australia, know now that the warders in transportation days were a thousand times lower and more degraded than the helpless men they flogged and maimed. Many writers have done research work on the ancient records, and Marcus Clarke (the librarian who kept the records!) wrote a magnificent novel,[1] showing only too clearly that the transportation-warders were the most degraded criminals in the whole world.

So it is a hard choice for the Antipodean with an ancestry. Unless he carries an Irish-sounding name, when he can point to the fact that enormous numbers of good Irish people were in fact transported to Australia in the early days of the nine-teenth century.

Of course, that much is well known nowadays. It is all over and done with, and one may write about the early days of the Irish struggle without arousing bad blood any more. The simple truth is that it was extremely easy for an Irishman to get transported, early in the nineteenth century. Almost as easy as it was for a wagon-man.

At first glance it might seem that those last two sentences were not connected. But they are really. Because a big percentage of the convict and ex-convict population of early Australia were romani people. Furthermore, many of those with Irish names were in fact wagon-folk. Kelly and Duane are not real Irish names. Nor Kieran, nor Tuohy, nor Colin. They are all names of tinker-clans, romani people most of them, some, perhaps, older than the romani. .

A great many of them lived in Ireland, or came and went between Ireland and Scotland like the Fays. So that those who were in Ireland in the 'troubled times' about the year 1800 were doubly unlucky. By the laws of England they were

[1] *For the Term of his Natural Life* (Macmillan, 1935).

liable to transportation anyway, as rogues and vagabonds and wandering thieves. If they happened to be swept into the net as Irish rebels also—that was so much the worse for them!

One result is that the mingling of those two breeds, in Australia of later days, produced a stamp and brand of men physically and mentally alert, courageous and resourceful, a breed who in the present writer's opinion will one day manage the whole world—and so much the better for the world.

Yet nothing could have been farther apart, in the early days before the transportation, than the Irish rebels and the wagon-borne romanis. Not even the most innocent houseman would expect a wagon-clan to mix themselves up in anyone's politics, certainly not in a vague struggle like the Irish rebellions which took place generation after generation.

By and large, the wagon-man does not take sides in any gorgia dispute, whether with guns or otherwise. Mostly he prefers to turn an honest pound from either side, in the way of fair dicker and trade. But none of that would save him in Ireland, any more than it saved him in England during the same period. From there comes the Say of Colin Colin.

There have always been plenty of caravan-folk in Ireland, and there were plenty of them in 1800 or thereabouts. The Colins were a big clan, ranging Mayo and the west country, down as far as the edge of Athlone, on the Shannon, but not south of there because of the Tuohy, with whom they always quarrelled.

Mayo and the west part of Ireland is a poor country, one of the poorest in the world, with only rocks and sand for soil, and hardly enough grazing for a farmer's horses, let alone the horses of a wandering tribe. In Ireland you may guess the nature of a district from the catch-phrase used when the place is mentioned. Mayo's catch-phrase tells poverty.

People speak of the Tipperary stone-throwers, because the Tipperary men have for centuries been good at putting the shot (originally with a big stone). Naming the county Kildare, the peasants will call it "short grass." There is a huge plain over most of Kildare, where the many horses, of wagon-people and others, have cropped the grass clean as a billiard table. Even to-day it is still the same, and people say "Kildare: short grass" automatically.

In the same way a Wexford man is called "Yellowbelly," not from any imputation of cowardice, but because of a famous breed of trout. Every district in Ireland, as in Scotland, has its descriptive phrase, but when we mention the western county we say "Mayo: God help us."

Mayo, God help us. It is enough to tell that the district is not a rich one, even for those who own things there, let alone for a wandering wagon-tribe. But that was the Colin country.

In the time about 1800 there would be even less to pick up than now. There would be no collecting of rags—from a starving peasantry to whom a ragged shirt was a wedding-present. Nor was there any tatting, because tins were not yet invented. There would be no buying or selling of scrap-iron —for if a Mayo peasant found half of a rusty horseshoe he could live on it for nearly a day!

Picking up a living would be an all-time job for the Colin-kye. But, of course, they managed. There would be ways and means, open to them but closed to the more God-fearing and law-abiding peasantry—salmon from the lord's lakes, and pheasants from his woods, a small trade in horses, and a little blacksmith and tinsmith work.

But they would be hard times for the Colin-kye neverthe-less, until the father of Colin Colin discovered a wonderful 'lark.' A lark is a way of life, a trade, practice, or occupation. The Colin leader's lark was the discovery that good hard money was being thrown away in the ditches by the starving peasants. Or if not good hard money, then things that could soon be dickered into the same, such as long leather top-boots, straps, and pouches, and even tall muzzle-loading guns.

At that time, and for long before, the British had been fighting against the Irish more or less continuously. And at one period the British were using European mercenaries, the

Hessians, the same which had also been used against the Americans. The Hessians were the troops of the Landgrave of Hesse, hired out to any country that wanted them, and they were supposed to be almost invincible. But, of course, they were not, as they found out to their cost against Washington's men at Trenton, in America, and against the O'Byrnes of Wicklow, and on the bog roads of Mayo, God help us.

At the time Colin Colin was a young man dead Hessians were thick as blackberries in the ditches of Mayo. And the frightened peasantry left them there, until maybe they were buried by the British and maybe not. But naturally a clan like the Colin-kye, coming the road in their wagons, would find other uses for a dead Hessian.

He nearly always had a long pair of leather top-boots on him, plainly worth good money. Also he generally carried a bullet-pouch, and leather straps, which were not cheap in those days, and very often a gun, one of the old muzzle-loaders. Wealth, in fact, lying by the roadside, because the Irish never touched the dead Hessians.

The Colins did. They went out and scoured the countryside after a shooting to look for dead Hessians in the ditches, and they took the top-boots and the guns and straps, until they had a wagon-load of each.

Robbing the dead, in plain language, and English people or Irish people would not like it, naturally. But, also naturally, a romani boy's outlook is different. All gorgia are the same to him, and for him there is no more desecration about taking a dead soldier's boots than there would be in taking the saddle off a dead horse. In fact the Colin-kye never once thought of anything except that they had a good lark. So young Colin Colin looked like coming to be a well-off man presently, instead of scratching a poor living along the bare bog roads of Mayo, God help us.

Then one day the Colin wagons pulled in on a quiet common west of the Shannon, and they had a counting of guns and saddles and straps and top-boots. Three wagon-loads they had all told, and now the next thing was to sell them. So next morning young Colin Colin pulled out, with his own living-wagon and three loaded vans behind him, and headed for Athlone, the nearest civilized town.

Unfortunately for Colin, Athlone was held by the British, and the first thing he knew was that a gun-muzzle was at his chest, and a circle of English soldiers was round his rake of wagons. Mystified, seeking only a fair dicker, he saw his wagons searched, and found himself in chains in a dungeon inside the Castle of Athlone.

And a marvellous capture it must have seemed, a whole munition-train no less, with guns and equipment galore, all captured from the rebel Irish. A marvellous capture! Of course, young Colin was lucky not to be shot out of hand, but he knew nothing of that, and was still mystified when he found himself shipped on a convict hulk bound for Australia, transported for life as an Irish rebel leader.

A romani, and a Colin, one who would hesitate before lifting one finger in any gorgia quarrel, English or Irish, transported as a rebel leader! It was a great irony, but naturally young Colin would not see the joke.

Then at Dover, while they were waiting for the ship to take them over the seas, there was further mystification. The convict ship was full of Irish and romani men, with a sprinkling of poor devils who had been in the Navy or the Army and were now transported for being poor devils. There were village poachers by the dozen, and young apprentices by the score, and servant girls who had stolen or had not stolen as much as threepence, and one unfortunate weeping child who had lost a latchkey.

There were nine brothers called Kelly, all wagon-men from County Clare, two of the Tuohys from Limerick, five of the Fays out of Scotland, Baillies and Browns and Bosivels from up and down England, with Kierans and Duanes besides, who were also tinker-men from Ireland, and a whole string of Irish gorgia, with names like O'Connell and O'Flaherty and O'Donohoe.

But the highwaymen and bank-robbers, the burglars and murderers, Colin Colin had expected to see were not there. How could a wagon-man from Mayo, God help us, know that the real criminals made their peace with the law in one way or another, as they did in Chicago of a later day, or know that the chief criminal of England was also the chief of the London police, Jonathan Wild?

A wagon-man is keen and sharp in many ways, and can survive where we from the houses will perish, but as an out-dweller Colin Colin could make no guess at the why and wherefore of city men. So he was again thoroughly mystified to find that most of those in the convict hulk were considerably more innocent than he was—he regarding himself as an innocent and much-wronged man!

There was, indeed, in the forward prison-hold of the ship, only one English criminal. Of course, Colin had heard about such things in the says, heard that the convict hulks contained mostly innocent romani people and a few simpleton gorgia from Ireland. But naturally he had taken it as slightly exaggerated. Now the presence of the one London criminal was so strange that among themselves the convicts called him English Bob!

This particular English Bob rose swiftly to be a warder, and lived a life of crime—as an official—in Australia, bringing misery and death to thousands of wretched convicts. His story is well known, and he has been referred to by writers like Marcus Clark, the Earl of Birkenhead, and others.

But for young Colin Colin the chief thing was that he was being transported in a convict ship on which there appeared to be *no* convicts, only the Fays and Duanes and Tuohys and a few Irish gorgia for whom he had the most supreme contempt. Those, with the Kellys and Kierans and the rest, were not what he had been expecting, in spite of the says. So he was able to scrape up a twisted laugh when one of the Kellys made a joke about the name of the ship. She was called *Success*.

In the say the old Colin-women will give in Cumberland or

Kent, or down in Mayo, God help us, all that is taken for granted. But naturally no reader would understand such a say without having the background explained. Only a writer like Charles Reade, or the late Earl of Birkenhead, or the modern novelist Philip Lindsay would grasp all the facts and appraise them properly. The old women simply assume that a transportation-ship around 1800 contained a few hundred innocent wagon-people and Irish, with a sprinkling of servant-girls who had quarrelled with their mistresses or apprentices who had stolen fourpence or lost a key.

So you may think what it was like when they showed Colin Colin the name on the ship, and read it out for him, and the name was *Success*. Because like all his people young Colin believed most fully that what a man had to come had to come, and now by a curious twisting road indeed he had come to success, with the Fays and the Kellys and Duanes, and many another fine romani man of whom he had heard for years. Success, although he was in chains, and bound over the seas.

Well, in Australia it was a testing-time, and in the earliest days they broke them and killed them, the soft poor English gorgia from the towns, poor people who had never slept out of doors one night, or ridden a horse one tenth part of a mile, or even stolen a rabbit or pheasant. How could they stay living, against the flogging and the tortures? How stay living, when a man could be hung for scowling at English Bob, or even for not scowling?

But, of course, the romani boys stayed alive, that knew bits of trickery from the woods and the moorland. And the English poachers stayed alive, too, that knew the ways of nature and of wild things. And a rake of the fighting Irish, who had starved so badly that they could starve no further, and knew tricks of going about from their life on the mountains and bogs, they stayed alive too.

Now, in Australia in those days the one thing the soldiers were sure of was that no one could run away. For there was nowhere to run, only out into a wild forest where men died of hunger in a few days, or where the blacks cooked them and ate them, or where the sun dried them up until they came back offering to be flogged for half a day if only the gaolers would give them a drink of water. There is many a say about it, many a say.

But the wild forest may frighten a poor London apprentice, or a houseman who never saw grass, and may still look good to the black Fays from the Border, or the Tuohy and Kelly people from the Irish mountains, or to an English village poacher. So they got together, the *Success* men, those of them who were left alive after one year, and in a body they downed the warders and soldiers, grabbed a gun or two, and took to the bush.

Death it was supposed to be. Certain death. For never before had anyone stayed alive in that bush, but was eaten by the blacks or thirst-driven back to the gaol-fence. But not the wagon-men from Scotland, and the English poachers, and the eight Kelly brothers who were still left alive out of the nine, and not the Tuohys or Colin Colin. They swept across that bush, a gang of bushrangers three hundred strong, with eighty of the women convicts who had chosen certain death, and they did not die.

The middle part of the say can be short, for it is known in the gorgia towns all over the world, and was in all the gorgia newspapers, and in a hundred books of printed words. Far from dying, they throve—the Kelly Gang, as the warders and soldiers called them in fear and trembling. Throve and robbed and fought and loved, married and bred children and fought the Government men by day and by night, fought them and beat them for twenty-two years. The Kelly Gang—but it was really Colin Colin at the head of a well-harnessed tribe of romani-men, with village poachers from England and a few of the hardiest of the rebel Irishers, those who had starved in the mountains of Mayo and could starve no more, but thrive on plenty, even in the bush of Australia.

So they went on, Colin Colin and the Duanes, with the

Fays and the Tuohys and the English poachers, never expecting that any one of them would ever see the sky over England or Ireland or Scotland again. For twenty-two years they went on, and Colin Colin had eleven tall sons, out of a girl of the Fays who had chosen certain death in the bush, and the Kellys were nearly a hundred people now, and the English poachers were stronger than ever, multiplying fast through the years, far more than the soldiers could kill.

Hard gold money Colin had, and horses by scores, wild horses of Australia that the romani boys had tamed, and sheep by the million if he wanted them, and enough rabbits to make a man think he was mad, especially if he had had to walk ten miles of a hard road to trap one lone rabbit back in Mayo. He had everything, but sometimes he knew black sadness for the feel of the wagon-wheels under him on an Irish road. Only that, of course, could never be, so this instead—his being a rich bushranger chief—was the success that was laid out for him.

Then one day the Government men gave a say that there would be no more transportation, and the bushrangers could come in or stay out if they liked, and all was forgiven!

Of course, Colin and the rest thought it was a trap. There had been such traps before, through the twenty-two years. But it was no trickery, only the truth in printed words from the Government. So it was not long before the Kellys and Colins and Tuohys swept down into Sydney, with all their people and all their gear, to look for ships back to England. Some stayed behind, because they liked Australia now, when they did not have to fight for every free breath. But Colin Colin made hot-foot across England and across Ireland, to the Bridge of Athlone, from which he started twenty-three years earlier.

Eleven tall Colins there were, his sons, with their wives and chavos, a troop of brumby horses worth maybe twelve thousand pounds, seven fine painted wagons that had been bought from the Fays in England, and Colin and his wife behind in their own kushti vado, coming home from his transportation.

Whatever a man has to come has to come, and it was a strange way Colin Colin came to success, on the ship *Success*, the convict ship.

That is the fantastic story of good luck that the old Colin women tell, in pride and awe, by the fires in County Mayo or round Derwentwater in England. For the rest, the others who stayed behind in Australia, there was similar or even greater good fortune, when transportation and almost certain death were changed into a lifetime of happiness, with freedom and wealth at the end.

Kelly and Duane and Colin—or Collins, as they call it in Australia—Kieran and Flaherty and O'Donohoe, with here and there a name like Holder or Harker—the Australians have them still, in plenty. But no Australian need be ashamed to claim that his progenitors were *not* respectable warders. Not if he carries one of the names listed here. His people were bush-rangers, the clan of a crowd of romani runaways, and Irish rebels, and English poachers (from whom come the Holder and Harker names), a crowd who ran away to certain death, into the bush, and survived.

Is it any wonder that one of the most famous ballads in Australia is also one of the best-known ballads among the northern wagon-men of England, and among the Irish in the west:

> ". . . for I'd rather roam the mountains wild
> Like a wolf or a kangaroo
> Before I'll slave for your Government men,"
> Said Bold Jack Donohoe.

Donohoe was one of the Kelly Gang, one of Colin Colin's men. Success comes often along a winding road, to show up where least expected.

The Conquest of Britain

ABOUT a hundred years before the present book was written, a Scottish writer named Simson produced a book called *The History of the Gipsies*. It is a most valuable work for any student.

Blinded by prejudice, terrified of the romani people, totally incapable of sympathy with his subject, Simson nevertheless had exceptional opportunities for observation of the travelling-folk in Scotland. Wherefore, in spite of the author's handicaps, the book is an outstanding one.

True, it contains all the old fantastic lies and guesses, the things which have been written by every people about some one or other. The story that a romani man has to drink his wife's urine on his marriage-night is there. Also the story that the wagon-men worship a dead horse. Things like that. But, in his straightforward reporting of things seen and heard by himself, the author performed a worthy work.

One will find in his book—from the other end, as it were —Torry Fay's story about the Gaberlunzieman. Except that Simson writes in stern rebuke of the fact that King James liked to go roaming the roads, and made a treaty with the Fays! There is also a valuable analysis of romani population and occupation in Fifeshire and the adjoining counties.

Now, Simson was frightened almost to death at the thought of what the gipsies would do to him when he published his book. He did in fact flee to America, and concealed his manuscript for twenty years. Because he thought the Fays or the Colins would kill him when they read it.

(One can imagine the reaction of Torry Fay's grandfather when he heard of the work—if he ever did. So far from killing poor Simson, the Fay elder would be much more likely to seek out his house, praise him most fulsomely for his wonderful print-paper say, guarantee that it was all true—and borrow a trifle of silver for the road.)

The chief reason for Simson's fear was a discovery he made about the romani. Mixed up with the myths and the crude obscenity suggestions and the foolish falsehoods is one piece of genuine research. It was for this that Simson thought his life was in danger.

His discovery was a simple one. Working over his comparative tables of population, he found out that romani people live a long time. Side by side with that went another discovery—namely, that they have a great many children. Later came the observation that what we now call infant mortality was very low among the travelling people. Most of the children stayed alive, grew up to be men and women.

At that stage Simson went frantically to work, checking up on the figures relating to the existing road-populace. He discovered, as anyone who has read the first chapter would expect, that the number of road-folk did not increase, was always at about the same level, few more and few less.

Then Simson asked himself—where do all the gipsies go? He recoiled in horror from the answer. Then he spent three years on a further investigation, found that his answer was the right one, wrote his book, and fled to America with the manuscript—before the Fays got him!

His answer was that the 'gipsies' have been and are being assimilated, that even the noblest families have 'gipsy' blood in them, *and that a wagon-man or wagon-woman never forgets the tribe.* So that, as far as the unfortunate writer was concerned, the whole of British civilization had been undermined by the romani, who were now part and parcel of British social life, but remained romani nevertheless.

Simson cleared out, concealed his manuscript, and died in America. Twenty years later his son published the book, adding an equal amount of his own material. Unfortunately, the son turned the book into a spiteful attack on the romani people, thereby spoiling much of his father's work, but the main argument, and the wealth of observation on which the argument was based, survive in spite of the ill-treatment. Of course, the elder Simson was right.

Among the wagon-people men breed until they are seventy or over. Women produce children until well past forty. Furthermore, the girls marry at a very early age. And there is no birth-control.

Thus the average family among road-folk is very much bigger than the average town family. Simson's population-increase tables are startling. But, without accepting them, it is still safe to say that a wagon pair will often produce and bring up to maturity nine or ten healthy children.

Yet the number of Lambs and Fays, of Grays and Bosivels and Colins, has never increased, as far as can be computed, since about the time of Queen Elizabeth.

Where are they all?

In an earlier chapter we heard a hypothetical Labour Exchange official say that gipsies are not reliable factory personnel. If a surplus million romani have come off wagon-wheels since the elder Simon's day it may be taken for granted without discussion that they have not found their way into the factories. Nor would one look for them in the Civil Service, they being mostly illiterate to start with!

Nor are they agricultural workers. Knowing every county

M

of England and Ireland from side to side, I have never met a single romani farm-labourer. They will be found at seasonal work like fruit-picking, but these are people from the road, and they go back to the road.

Then where are the others? Already we have one clue, in the reference to their absence from the Civil Service. One need only look for them in environments where a strong personality and native shrewdness may bring wealth and influence even without formal education.

Take Simson's bogy first, the queen bee from his bonnet. Simson's dread and fear and horror came from a fixed belief that the romani had 'got themselves into' the aristocracies of Scotland and England. He cites numerous instances of a romani man under sentence of death having been saved at the last minute by the intervention of some titled lady or her lord.

One case he mentions is of a travelling-man who was sentenced to death on no fewer than three occasions, being saved each time when the lord of the manor stepped in on his side. The author hints darkly that the mother or grandmother of the noble lord was a wagon-woman, and that the didicai never forget their own.

Nowadays no one would care. But it must be remembered that since Simson's time we have passed through the rigid conventionalism of Victorian days, at the very beginning of which era the author lived. Of course, he regarded, and had to regard, such histories with outraged propriety and respectable horror.

For him the worst feature of the case was that the romani who had risen in the world did *not* forget the tribe. Presumably in his view the hero of the Liltie Hearn say would have been Liltie, and the villains the Bosivels!

But times have changed. Simson, and Queen Victoria, are dead. It is no longer necessary to praise decent Liltie Hearn, who got on in the world and took care to cut himself adrift from his low beginnings and his former friends of the road. At present the chief interest is in the fact that Simson *has* picked on one environment where a person may be rich and powerful—without being greatly troubled by a lot of silly book-learning.

There is no real need to follow up all Simson's dark hints and veiled suggestions. Two or three well-authenticated cases exist of a noble family boasting that they had a romani ancestor or ancestress. There was a famous and beautiful Lady Lovell in the seventeenth century who came straight off the road. But, alas for poor Simson, her descendants boast of it instead of hiding it!

The old Scots author's real grievance was the 'remembrance' —the tribal solidarity, as we should call it to-day. It is very real; otherwise there would be no story about Hearn, the exception. A dozen times the old writer comes back to the romani mother, now a titled lady, teaching her children what he contemptuously calls "their wonderful story." Every time he puts the phrase into quote-marks, as if it were somehow criminal for a mother to tell her children that their ancestors came over with William the Conqueror—or travelled the roads of France before the Conqueror was born.

Prolonged and shrewd observation led the old Scot to write at length about one tremendously interesting fact—namely, the essential and almost hermit-like frugality of the romani people. He refers—with scorn—to the fact that many a titled lady in Scotland could leave the comfort of her opulent home and drink tea from a battered jar by a roadside fire with her own people. He mentions the ease with which the aristocrat of road-origins can drop back into wearing rags or sleeping in a crowded tent.

All this is anathema to him. Because it shows, as he saw it, that you never really *have* the gipsy. He or she really belongs to the road, and can go back there at a moment's notice. Wherefore the telling of the "wonderful story" is a graver crime still—since it would be paving the way for the children to do likewise!

Simson must have had dreadful nightmares. But at any rate

he pointed out one field in which a road-person might be wealthy and influential without knowing much of the print-paper lore. It might be well to look at the other end of the social scale, at the people who leave the road-slums, the crabby wagons.

They will not be marrying into the aristocracy. But neither will they be drifting into factory-life, because they are mentally and physically unfit for it, incapable of surviving as ordinary honest workers. Nor are they qualified to be criminals, although some few of them do in fact drift to the lowest levels of petty crime, to finish with long gaol-sentences for crude and trivial law-breaking.

Generally they keep to the edges of the big cities, to the slum outskirts which verge every industrial centre, and engage in puny, blundering 'business.' Little coal-dealers, little firewood-sellers, little carriers, with perhaps a few shillings in vegetable-huckstering—these are their trades, and one may spot their road-origins without reading the names on their trolleys or vans.

But each of these categories, the high and the low, takes only a small number of the romani who leave the road. For the remainder, the majority, one must still look in fields where an income may be earned—the bigger the better—by one shrewd in the ways of the world but lacking formal education. We have a second clue already, even from the road-slum people; the wagon-men come into civilization on its edges, in the trades and professions where book-culture is not only unnecessary but may be a handicap.

The process is natural, gradual, and inevitable, as will easily be seen when one gives the matter a second's thought. Suppose a romani couple engaged in horse-trading have seven sons, five of whom might be horse-traders themselves if there were an 'opening.' There will be no opening. When the boys are grown men their home district will still only support two horse-traders—and their parents are still alive, only started, as the old woman might put it in the Syety Say. Suppose the five sons will not become factory men, cannot enter any occupation requiring book-learning, and are not sufficiently wealthy to start in new businesses of their own. What then?

They take the next best line, which is really the same line, and move with the times. Horses are becoming fewer, motors are replacing them, motor-trading (car-coping, it might almost be called!) does not call for a vast culture. Large numbers of the former horse-dealers became motor-traders.

In any pub round Great Portland Street, in London, the chief car-mart district, one might almost close one's eyes and fancy it was the horse-fair of Barnet or the dealing-green at Stow-on-the-Wold or the horse-market of Beccles. It is the same trade, and in many cases they are the same people, moving with the times.

And neither do *they* forget the road or the road-folk. Around Great Portland Street there are many places where a man buying a car, even if he only had wagon-wheels behind him on his mother's side, would get a clean cut of the whip and a fair dicker. Old Simson would be horrified, but surely it is a good thing for a man to remember his origins if they be not shameful.

Some of the other occupations are obviously suitable, *par excellence*, for romani folk who have left the road. All those, for example, in which the fairground was the half-way stopping-place.

People with names like Heath, Wood, Bosco, Colin, Copsey, Spinner, Forrest, and so on may be proud, if they like, that their forbears came off the road. They are all romani names. In fact, they are all the same name, because Bosco and Forrest and Wood and Spinner mean nearly the same thing, and in many languages Colin simply means a little wood.

But every one of those names will be found in the show business. There must be a dozen Woods, each managing his own boxing-show—one acting as a boxing-promoter in a big way. Collins and Forrest are the names of two very wealthy families, covering every branch of showmanship between them. Bosco the elder was a pioneer in little theatres, originally on fairgrounds at a penny a time under canvas!

But perhaps the most surprising of what may be called the respectable middle-class fields of free enterprise, in which the romani people were not only participants but pioneers, is the film industry. Who on earth would expect an illiterate wagon-man to turn up as an initiate and an adept in the most modern and sophisticated occupation in the world? Who but the elder Simson! But in they came, off the roads and the fairgrounds, and, indeed, via the fairgrounds.

It happened but yesterday, or only a generation ago, and many of the people are still alive. But the townsmen forget, or do not know. The film industry started in tents at country fairs, long before there was any such thing as a "picksher-palace." Indeed, the first cheap picture-houses were an attempt to bring the fun of the fair, the country film show, within the reach of town working-people.

Anyone in the film business knows about the Bosco film shows—twopence standing room—in country fairs. Soon the Bosco show was a big marquee instead of a tent, and only then Bosco moved into the towns. Lijah Shaw was another pioneer who showed films for pennies at fairs in the early days. (Incidentally, Shaw is still *another* word like Copsey and Bosco and Wood; they come with strange regularity.)

Presently the entrepreneurs discovered, as they were bound to do, that films need not necessarily be bought or even hired from the gorgia. Films could be made. Most certainly they could be made by any man with a thousand-year background of using tools of every kind. That is, as far as the practical side of the trade was concerned.

So the tent-film exhibitors moved into Wardour Street, in among the city men who knew the trade. In the reminiscences of any British film-producer those early ones take a large part. Some of them are but recently dead, and some of them are still alive (road-folk live a long time). It is safe to say that they engaged, and some of them made fortunes, in every single branch of the film business—exhibition, distribution, production, direction, and script-writing.

That last item might sound fantastically out of place, when one speaks of people many of whom could not read their own names. But it is a fact. Some of the early film-scripts were turned out by fairground men who could hardly write a postcard.

But after all it was only another variation of the 'tale'! It was easy for natural story-tellers. There is one other interesting and amusing consideration; many of the early British films were about horses or horsemen.

The didicai were running true to type.

It was twice my own privilege to work with a film man on outdoor films in which his first-hand knowledge of horses and dogs saved his company many thousand pounds. In theory his employees were supposed to look after such things. In fact, he handled every emergency himself—although he was not supposed to know anything about the subjects.

He could work as a projectionist, and show a film, could photograph one if necessary, and cut the negative if he had not a cutter. He could direct a film, large or small, had directed many and earned big money. He could produce a film—and write the script himself if necessary.

His name was Cooper.

Significantly enough, the biggest film he ever made, one considered a marvellous job of cinema-work even to-day, was about Claude Duval the highwayman. The shots of horsemanship are still spoken of with pleasure among cinema-men. Cooper devised them himself, and directed them himself.

In the other fields allied to the showground, that is, among film-actors, singers, and dancers, the brown-faced, black-eyed people with the road-names are well represented. In an earlier chapter I referred to the coincidence that Gary Cooper's name was straight romani. There are many such coincidences.

Some of the people have the sense to boast of it. It has even reached the stage where non-romani folk try to cash in on the road-background! But the city people who patronize theatres and cabarets soon find out. It would be easier for a fox to pretend it was a rabbit.

One would not look for a romani doctor, lawyer, or editor. The dice are too heavily loaded. That is, against the first generation off the road. Of course, the son of a man who made money in cars or films might make a splendid advocate, having many a thousand years of training in mental agility built into his very fibres. But so far the romani are unrepresented in those professions.

In the advertising world, on the other hand, the road-names come as thick and fast as they do in the little theatres, and for the same reason. Advertising is a new industry, only one stage removed from the fairground, via the old fly-posting, nearly all of which was done by romani people in process of settling down.

So it goes. From high to low, from castle to slum, the overflow of the romani people have come into civilization during the last two hundred years. Seldom or never do they come as workmen, because they are unreliable when working for a daily wage under a master. Which is natural enough. They have a long race-history of being their own masters, even in a very poor way.

Generally they look for some field where they can be their own masters, or nearly so, as in all the cases mentioned here. Gluttons for work, they slave as only those can slave who know the delights of laziness.

But poor old Simson was right. They never forget the "wonderful story." Why should they?

Wherefore the conquest of Britain appears to have come about exactly as it was forecast and feared by the author of *Gipsy History*. But who cares?

England has been conquered—and unconquered again—a dozen times, has assimilated her conquerors, taken their best and made it better. If the invasion of the last two hundred years is a fact, it is none the worse for having come without fire and sword. It saves time in the assimilation!

Who does not know them, in any walk of English life, the dark-eyed people with the soft voices, the tall, full-bosomed women with the fine complexions, the pixy children with the black hair? The lean, shrewd-eyed trader with the humorous smile, the slim and healthy incredibly wrinkled ancient women —they are in every suburb nowadays. Maybe they do not come from the road but only look like it!

But the young married women at any rate are unmistakable. Lithe and lovely, with clear dark eyes that can look back down a million miles of road, they know the facts and practice of life and love, know how to love their men without having to learn from a Sunday newspaper. Different they are, a new thing in the suburban streets, and when they are assimilated the suburbs will be the better for it.

No one in these days will name it an outrage that such mothers should tell their children the wonderful story. Nor that they should be hermit-frugal instead of bloated and blowsy, should be able at a minute's notice to share a tent again or ride a wagon. Old Simson was right, only his dreaded 'conquest' is not a tragedy but an awakening.

CHAPTER SEVENTEEN

The Rout-i-tou

IN a small thatched tavern on the outskirts of Stow-on-the-Wold I sat and drank hard black rum with Plingro Ria. He had other names on his papers, and therefore Plingro was not his legal designation. But it was the romani equivalent of the name on his identity-card, and a man may use the Scots or Irish equivalent of his name without harming anyone, so why not the wagon-name as well?

As is usual among the romani people, and many peoples of Europe, the surname comes first, so that a man will be called Smith Harry or Bosivel Simon. Plingro does in fact mean Smith, and is better known to many readers when spelt in its full form of Petulengro. In the case of a polysyllabic name like Serpengro, Petulengro, and the rest, the romani people tend to cut away the word to its bare rudiments, so the names become Spingro and Plingro. Plingro Ria would be called Henry Smith in town fashion.

He sat and drank the rum, and talked about roads. The tavern was packed, as the horse-market was on, and the licensing laws with regard to closing-time are temporarily suspended on such days. In the big taproom ten different crowds sat round tables, and drank, and talked horses and horse-trading without end.

There was a continual coming and going. From time to time one group or another broke up and the people went back to the horse-market, only to return a few minutes later to drink again and haggle over new horses and new prices.

The people who owned the tavern were kept busy hurrying to and fro with trays of drinks, sweating while they reaped a rich harvest, for every one drank a great deal, and only two or three times a year would their taproom be so packed, only two or three times a year would the law permit them to stay open all day. Laughing and jovial, they took the big money and plied the drink to the continually changing groups.

At one table three farmers, a horse-dealer, and a lean jockey-like man conducted a loud argument which necessitated much slapping of palms, many protestations of integrity, and an endless wrangle about such items as 'the splitting of the odd fiver.' Round another table half a dozen lorry-drivers, who had driven in the big motor horse-boxes, drank and talked roads while they waited for orders. In a corner four hard-looking, well-dressed men exchanged monosyllabic phrases, made entries in little notebooks, and handled huge rolls of notes. Near them three grooms, casual horse-handlers, listened eagerly, exchanging nods and muttered comments as the destination of each bunch of horses was fixed. A girl in gaily coloured gipsy clothes sat on the corner of a table and laughed at the haggling groups near her. A small child sat on the floor in a corner and drank its father's beer while he was busy.

Another and larger table held three groups widely different in dress, and holding no communication with one another. One of the groups was obviously a family, consisting of a woman and her husband, two young men, and a young woman. All were poorly dressed, except for the kushti diklos, the expensive neck-scarves, each tied in the same intricate pattern of knots that showed the family were wagon-people, and Smiths. Beside them three men and a young woman, all well dressed and of business-like appearance, talked in low tones and ignored the gipsies. Still lower down on the same table two stout men, like prosperous bookmakers or auctioneers, ignored the other two groups as they discussed horses and prices.

In the middle of the room a young obvious romani, of fifteen or sixteen, was already very drunk, talking maudlin inconsequentialities to the three young farmers and a country horse-dealer with whom he had been drinking. Two girls like typists sat alone, sipping glasses of sherry and looking round avidly at the strange scene. An old woman went from table to table, wishing good luck to the seller at the end of each concluded deal, accepting the florins and half-crowns that came her way as a matter of course.

And by my own table a lean brown youngster wearing a Smith-knotted diklo watched me with predatory eyes, glanced appraisingly each time I reached for money to pay for a drink, caught my eyes and smiled in friendly fashion two or three times, until Plingro Ria gave an infinitesimal headshake and he transferred his attentions to a half-drunken farmer.

The groups came and went, disintegrated and reformed, as the horse-market passed through its various stages. Twice or three times Plingro Ria and I went out into the street, and across to the big yard where the market was held, Smith to stop for a few hurried words at each little group by the gates and corners.

None of that was strange to me, since it is the ordinary routine of an Irish horse-fair, although it is seldom encountered in England. People have to know things from minute to minute if they are to make money, whether their profession involves the investment of a thousand pounds in variegated horse-flesh or the acceptance of half-a-crown pourboire from some one who has just completed a satisfactory deal.

Who considers he has paid too much for that last lot of colts, and will "put them in again after dinner"? Who has

bought twice as many horses as he expected, and will be frantic
to hire horse-boxes before evening? Who has a big bunch
for a lonely district, and will need many horse-handlers, almost
at their own price?

Who has £660 in fivers on him, and is drunk and in generous
mood?

Things like that. As the Stock Exchange has its ticker-tape,
the horse-market has its grapevine. But in and around Stow-
on-the-Wold all the people on the grapevine that particular
afternoon seemed to be Smiths. Plingro Ria was the go-
between, the telephone exchange, as it were. So we were in
and out of the tavern many times.

Then as the afternoon wore on the groups in the taproom
thinned. The country people from the outlying districts were
departing, the auctioneers' men were completing their books
and leaving, the lorry-drivers were being called for one by one.
Outside in the big pub yard cars were being pulled out under
an archway, horses were being harnessed to traps and gigs,
people were going home. But inside the taproom the drinking
had only just commenced in earnest.

Half of the room was empty, and all the remaining people
had drawn more closely together at a line of tables all along
one side of the room. Three of the horse-dealers were there,
with one farmer and the lean jockey. Two grooms and a
ragged horse-handler drank and talked with a man I had seen
spend over three thousand pounds in fifties and sixties during
the day. One of the typist-girls gossiped with a young fellow
like an auctioneer's clerk, and the romani family still kept
together, joined now by the youngster who had been maudlin
drunk but was now nearly sober. The predatory young man
sat opposite me, and drank with Plingro Ria and myself. All
the distinct and separate groups were still there, in cadre as it
were, but drawn more closely together now, at the line of
tables along one side of the room.

Gradually people from the various groups began to exchange
remarks with those in other groups near them, began to accept

or pay for drinks outside their own tables. Gradually it dawned on me that they knew one another much better than had at first appeared, and presently I felt convinced that I was the only real stranger present.

The thing was clinched when Plingro Ria bought a very big round of drinks. Previously the groups had been getting their own drinks in the ordinary way, each having five or six drinks at a time, for its own people at its own table. Plingro and I had never more than two or three people with us up to then, a young Smith or two, an occasional horse-dealer and so on, but generally only five or six people at the table, so that there was never need to pay for more than a few drinks at a time. But at this stage Plingro made a sign to the barmaid, said "Go along, sister," and waved down the room.

The girl fetched a huge tray of drinks, placing one before every person in the room. Each acknowledged it with a lift of the glass and a nod to Plingro.

When it was my turn I called the barmaid and ordered drinks for those at our table. Then I hesitated for a split second, and asked Plingro Ria, "Can I tell her to go along?"

"Do that, brother," he confirmed, with a grin. "Do that, and we'll see." I made the same wave of the hand and told the girl to go along. Again she fetched an enormous tray of drinks, putting one in front of each person, with an indication, as barmaids usually give, of the person who had sent it. There was a perceptible pause, a lull in the conversation.

The horse-handlers and grooms took their drinks at once, lifting their glasses to say, "Good luck, sir," as is usual. The people at our own table took theirs. One auctioneer's clerk held his glass uncertainly and looked at me with disapproval. The little typist held up her glass of sherry in an uncertain way, nodded shyly, and glanced away at once. The others, the horse-dealers and the romani men, sat and looked woodenly in front of them, apparently not understanding what had happened. I began to feel a dreadful fool.

Then Plingro Ria leant forward to ask me some trivial

question, something about whether I had his matchbox or not. He reached over to lay one large hand on my shoulder.

"You have the matchbox, prawla?" he inquired, and grinned while he waited for the matches. This is the word prale, meaning brother, the word usually spelt 'pal' in English.

The difference between being called 'Dear sir' by an income-tax man after his pound of flesh and being called 'Dear' by a person beloved is the same as that between being called 'brother' and 'prale' by a romani, although they are the same word. Five seconds after Plingro had asked for his matches every one relaxed.

The people drank, and laughed and drew closer, then set about finishing their business, the business which had been awaiting my departure. Adding and subtracting—in words—and the exchange of money went on all over the room. Each person was busy, perhaps paying fourteen pounds to one neighbour, receiving eleven from some one on the other side, arguing whether he owed forty-two or forty-one to a man at another table. Handfuls of banknotes were exchanged, and for ten minutes the place resembled a bourse or a bank rather than a taproom. Then every one drew a long breath, and the Smiths started in to enjoy themselves.

Loud, excited laughter and chatter filled the room. Invitations to drink passed on every hand. There was talk of roads among the Plingros who had not seen one another since last market-day, and gossip about absent members of the family. Then, a little later, after further drinking, some of the people began to sing.

Even if they were young people they sang the music-hall songs of fifty years ago. It was strange to hear the old ballads coming from youngsters whose fathers were not born when the songs were current. *Just like the Ivy on the Old Garden Wall*, *Two Little Girls in Blue*, *Only a Bird in a Gilded Cage*, and *Clementine* followed one another quickly. There were no Hollywood love-lyrics.

Then they went to older songs, road songs and ancient

ballads from the English countryside. They even sang *Down by those Green Bushes*, a song which I had believed known only to Irish wagon-people. Later some one sang a song with many strange words interpolated. The romani words were jerked out and very difficult to follow, but the song was apparently of Rabelaisian content, from the male guffaws after each interpolation.

The people were becoming more and more pleasurably excited, and there was a rhythmic rapping of glasses, and a calling of "Rout-i-tou; rout-i-tou." A young fellow jumped into the middle of the floor and began to step-dance, alone, and for a moment there was silence. He finished by kicking one foot very high, slapping his hands together below it while his leg was in the air, and at once the excited calls recommenced: "Rout-i-tou; rout-i-tou!"

Suddenly a girl jumped to the centre of the floor and began to step-dance very fast. After a few seconds she kicked her right leg very high, dropped her foot to the ground, and stood still. At once the calls of "Rout-i-tou" broke out again, and she stood silent until some one handed her a beer-bottle. She held the bottle upside down, letting it drain itself empty, then suddenly kicked her right foot upward to a great height.

Swiftly, and even while her right foot came to the ground, she passed the empty bottle across into her left hand, kicked her left foot towards the ceiling, and passed the bottle back again. The double movement was almost too fast for the eye to follow.

She continued the same dance-motion in a slow rhythm, and gradually all the tavern-company came on to beating time, with trays or glasses, or hand-clapping, or a castanet sound made by handfuls of money.

Imperceptibly the girl increased the speed of her kicking. Her short skirt flashed to and fro, to and fro, up and down, to and fro, as her hands continually sent the beer-bottle shuttling from side to side. Each kick was higher than the girl's head, every millimetre of her lissom body was in motion, and the continuous lightning-fast weaving of arms and legs made an incredibly attractive picture.

The accompaniment from the crowd was perfect in timing. Here a stout brown-faced matron beat the rhythm with a thick wedding-ring on a tin tray. There an old man rang two glasses together. Elsewhere the people beat time by throwing money from hand to hand—a splendid castanet effect simply achieved. And always the whole company chanted the unchanging refrain of "Rout-i-tou; rout-i-tou."

No dance from an African jungle, no hula-hula rhythm from a South Sea island, could have produced such an effect on a crowd. The sensuous allurement of the scene and the motion, the rhythm-born excitement, had worked the audience into an intoxication of pleasure. Then the girl stopped suddenly, and there was a roar of applause.

I myself had been as much excited as every one else, and probably showed it. Plingro Ria watched me with an appraising smile at the end of the dance.

"Nothing like that in Ireland, brother," he commented, laughing. Then he looked up in surprise when I nodded my head to contradict him.

"Plenty," I explained. "Not among road-folk either, but among peasant people. Only they don't pass a bottle or anything from hand to hand." Smith dismissed my remarks with a tolerant wave.

"Then there's nothing," he asserted. "You have to pass something from side to side—else it's like a loom without a shuttle, yes?" He looked at me, and smiled slowly. "Yes?" he repeated.

The rum was black and very strong. Also I had been a long time at the tavern. But I was sufficiently alert to know that I was being given a valuable lesson on the place of phallic symbolism in the terpsichorean art. I grinned, and kept silent, and strolled out to the big yard for a breath of air. Plingro came along, down the passage towards the outer door.

"The rout-i-tou doesn't get into your blood," he said

N

ruminatively. "It's *in* your blood. Every one's. Only in towns a man forgets, and that's all." He leant one hand on my shoulder, and laughed. "I am saying," he insisted, "that the birds in the hedges and the hares on the hills know the rout-i-tou. It brings luck in marriage, to animals or men."

"Come off that road, Ria," I ordered argumentatively. "Pull your horses, and stop boasting. Else you'll tell me the romani are the only people who know anything about love and marriage. Come off."

"Not the only ones, brother," grinned Smith, in slow good humour. "But anyone that has luck in marriage knows the rout-i-tou. And if you once have it you never lose it. Funniest say ever," he laughed, "was about——" He stopped, and turned away into the yard to see some one, and I waited until he was on his way back.

"That funny say?" I prompted him, as we steered our way back to the taproom. "About the——"

"Aye," said Plingro. "This was a romani man, that came rich and had a lovely house by the edge of London. A good boy. Of the best. So he's making four or five thousand a year, married with one of our own, a real beauty one, and they have rich noble friends, as would be right. Not to shame themselves, either, and be just rich people with no print-book words, but both well schooled, and fit to have a king to tea if they liked and not to be made look little.

"So when their dollcie ben burra friends came to stay, or to visit, they were the same lady and gentleman as anyone else, and good people. So it went on, years, and the two of them liked and loved by all, rich and nice with it besides.

"Then one evening they had friends to visit, art-kye and writers and such—you know what people, brother. So for their entertainment they had a small, curious, and very expensive orchestra, a Martinique band, made up of three young men. Maybe you've seen these Martiniques, brother, a gold-brown people and very gay. Could be quarter black, say, and quarter French, and maybe quarter romani, and another

quarter Spanish and likely a quarter Portugee and romani
again from that side. So they——"

"Here," I interrupted. "How many quarters in an orange
this afternoon, eh?"

"Maybe five, brother," grinned Plingro. "There'd be a lot
of romani in them Martiniques, from the Spanish side and the
Portugee, without the bit of straight wagon-wheel. Maybe
five, and that's what I'm telling you. These three could make
good string music, and they could dance in a way to quicken
the heart of a dying man. But there it was—they were men,
for one thing, and for another they had nearly the right
tap-a-tap but not quite, and for a third they danced with
nothing in their hands, but just danced.

"So it was good, and very good, but not just right. And at
the end of their big show-dance all the people clapped hands.
But you could feel that they'd only been lifted up, and then
put down again, cold-feeling. That meant you could feel
there was a little disappointment.

"Then suddenly there was a *whoo-oo* and a flutter of skirts.
And into the middle of the floor jumped the high rich lady
of the house, the society lady that was the hostess, the wife
of this romani-man. In she jumped, with her short skirt
flying high, and a wine-bottle in her hand, and danced the
rout-i-tou.

"They say it lifted her high rich visitors, until every one
thought they were young again—maybe two hundred years
younger—and that party and that visit was the biggest successful visit there was by the rich ones of London *that* year. The
nicest thing was that it did the pair no harm, but only good.
None of the high rich friends thought it was wrong or cheap-
say, but all believed it was art-kye learning, that maybe cost
her thousands of gold money to learn.

"Her having learnt it on the road, in places like this. It
brings good luck in marriage, I tell you, brother," insisted
Plingro.

Knowing he was right, I remained silent, and presently

Smith and I went out to walk in the now-quiet street. It was early evening, and a few street-lights were on.

The little country town was already almost deserted, quiet and somnolent after the bustle of the horse-fair. Peace, and snug comfort, and rural respectability had replaced the raucous clamour of the preceding hours. Nothing could have been farther removed from the primitive savagery of the scene at the tavern.

Plingro and I drew in big breaths of the clean air, and smelt the freshness of the little town. But we grinned together, and both turned to look back towards the tavern nevertheless. Then we sauntered into the little square which was also the bus-terminus, and a girl passed us without a hint of recognition as she boarded the Oxford bus.

It was the girl who had danced the rout-i-tou, the little typist, going back to her office in Oxford, after an afternoon among her own people.

They never *really* leave the road!

CHAPTER EIGHTEEN

Odyssey

WHEN the Kellys and the Colins were bushranging in New South Wales they were supposed to do many wicked things. But, of course, that was according to the gorgia papers, which would *have* to say the bushrangers were wicked. (All except one newspaper, which was edited by a brother of Donohoe the bushranger!)

Anyone who knows the truth knows that it would not have paid the bushrangers to do wickedness. They had to be friends with the countryside, of course, in the ordinary run of the road. But there was one thing they did which on any man's say was a wicked one, and they knew it. Wherever they went in New South Wales they enslaved the blacks, made them carry and haul, rounded them up like wild horses and put them to work like tame horses.

This was worse when it was done by romani men, who do not like to be forced into work for anyone. But there was one other side to it, not much of an excuse but an excuse. The blacks were always on the Government side.

When the Government men were out chasing a bushranger, instead of using bloodhounds to track him down they used

the black trackers. For years and years the black trackers had
run down every runaway, followed the line of him by little
broken twigs and bent blades of grass, smelt him and pointed
his way, found the tiny hidden marks of his feet, and run him
down for the floggers and the gallows.

All that, of course, was before the romani men and the
English poachers got out in the bush. Because these fellows
knew ten times more than any black, and could read ten times
more sign off the grass and twigs. So as soon as they swept out
bushranging then it was good-bye, black trackers, and they
were the hunted ones instead.

Now this will be hard to believe for people, that a man from
an English village, or a romani boy off the English roads,
should be better skilled in the ways of the wild than a black
man in the middle of the bush. But they were, and they are,
so that a person can understand about Two-Water Smith and
the way he set out to find a girl.

If you talk with a romani boy and you watch his eyes you
will see that he is running them over you all the time. Then
you wonder what for, and by the ordinary way of things you
never find out. But sometimes, if you come friendly, one will
tell you. He watches because he must, because he is trained
to use his eyes, like a fox or a weasel.

That romani boy will talk with you for two minutes by your
watch, answering your question about what time the bus goes
to Birmingham or wherever it is. Then if you meet him one
month later, and come friendly, he will be able to tell you
bits about how you looked that morning the last time he
saw you.

He will tell you that the nail on the little finger of your left
hand was broken, that one of your shoelaces had its tag trodden
on, that you were smoking a Players cigarette but had Wood-
bines in your pocket, that you had a little wheeze to your breath
because you had a cold that day, that the second button on
your jacket had been sewn on with grey thread instead of
brown, and that you'd been seeing a different girl, more or less

close, since the morning he spoke with you. Little things like that.

The poor black trackers! What chance had they?

Now, that was the kind of sharp-eyed one young Two-Water Smith was coming on to be, and him living less than thirty miles from the centre of London! He had the advantage of living near the big cities, because he could pop in and out, seeing pavements as well as roads, although he had never slept one night outside a wagon in his life.

A slim, wiry, good-looking black-faced young fellow, twenty-odd, his name on the road was Plingro Lem. But among the people of his own district he was called after the village near which he was born, a little place at the junction of small rivers, called Two Waters. So he was always Two-Water Smith, to separate him from Chipperfield Smith and Redburn Smith, people of the same family.

Living near civilized places, he had to be quicker on the take, quicker on the come and go, than a romani boy whose rake of wagons made their wend on a Yorkshire moor, for instance. Sometimes there would be a sour village constable, one who knew where a romani wagon might pitch, and who'd look the place over at nightfall to make sure there were no thieving didicai about. Things of that kind.

Then ten minutes after that village constable had gone home, certain that all was well, the wagon of Two-Water Smith would pull out from some track in the woods and haul into the pitch, sure of being unmolested, there of all places, until morning. And ten minutes before that constable came next afternoon Two-Water would be off, headed for some other sharp village constable ten or twelve miles away. That is how a romani boy has to go on, if he lives too near the big house-towns. But Two-Water always made out well.

Now one day up on the Berkhamsted Road the Smith wagon was halted by a burra ben rye, a rich, good-humoured gentleman. They have talk, and the rich man wants Two-Water Smith, with his horse and wagon, to make use of them in a film he is to make. The money would be good, and the film was to be made from a book called *Red Wagon*, and written by Lady Eleanor Smith.

Now, it could be ordinary enough for a rich titled lady to be called Smith. Also it could be ordinary for her to write a book. Besides, it *might* be ordinary for that book to be called *Red Wagon*. But not ordinary was it that the book should be a good one! Only it was. It said nothing wrong about the travelling-people, fairground folk, and the like, so Two-Water Smith could let his face and his wagon be used in it without having shame on the road. He took on to do it, and went over to the film studio in London.

The first night he went out from the centre of London, since he couldn't stay in his wagon in the film studio, and he stayed in the wagon of some friends out near Hemel Hempstead. Then he was late next morning when he got to the place, so they told him to stay in the city, which he did, for the rest of the time they were making the film.

So he was like a real houseman, an office gorgio, getting up each morning and hurrying off to work, then back to the hotel in the evening, and enjoying himself every minute of the time, so many strange things were to see and smell and hear, up and down London. Then one day when the film was nearly finished, out near Shepherd's Bush, where the film studio was, Two-Water Smith was walking out of the main studio gate, and a girl was walking in, and they swopped eyes, and Two-Water knew that one was his mort, gorgia or no gorgia.

He darted back into the studio entrance again, but, of course, the office gorgio stopped him, because you have to have a pass and a paper for each time you go in, and Two-Water's paper for that day had already been given up. So he waited outside, for maybe five hours, until the place was all locked up for the night, but the girl never came out. Then next day Two-Water found that there were several entrances, so he set out to find the girl again.

First he went to the office gorgio who had stopped him,

and asked about the girl, but of course the man gave him no help, since girls by the hundred or maybe the thousand came in and out of that gate. Then Smith went away, and thought things over, and walked up and down the streets of London for hours without finding any tracks.

No one is to think this one would be like a simple village boy, looking for one girl among millions and millions of people. Two-Water was looking for something that was a track, but did not find it, so he walked the streets again for every hour he was free.

Then the picture was finished, and Smith could go home, as the gorgia men put it, meaning that he could go back on his wagon-wend. But he stayed in London, with more time to walk about now. He was looking for a girl carrying the same kind of leather box he had seen with the girl at the studio, and at last he saw one, one evening getting off a bus.

"If I tell you a civil question, madam," says Two-Water, "will you say me the answer?" The girl looked at him, a pretty little thing and smart, and she smiled, because girls never found it hard to smile at Plingro Lem.

"Certainly," she said. "If it's not too—well, certainly. What is it?"

"You have a dark green leather box with a slanting top and a handle, weighing maybe sixteen pounds, and never kept out of doors," said Two-Water. "What is that box, madam?"

"You mean this," said the girl, holding it up. "This is a portable typewriter."

"Could you tell me," asked Two-Water, "what kind of girl would carry one of those portable typewriters? I mean, madam, what would she do for a living? What do you do, if I may tell you a civil question?" The girl smiled again.

"Certainly," she told him. "I'm a secretary in the City. Let me see," she went on, and thought for a moment. "Girls who'd carry a portable might be secretaries, or typists from an agency, or writers, or journalists, out on a job. That's all, I think."

"Your husband will be hated by all his men-friends," said Plingro Lem. "May I give you good luck for your civil say?" He went off, repeating the words the girl had used. Next morning he went out to Shepherd's Bush, and fronted the office gorgio.

"If a man was to tell you a civil question," he commenced, "would you say him a civil answer?"

"What's your business?" snapped the man. "I'm not here to answer questions." Two-Water smiled, and licked his lips a bit.

"If a man," he said pleasantly, "was to kick you in the middle, kind of hard, and then jump on your face, and gouge the two eyes out of your head before you hit the ground, and *then* offer to fight your fair, would he get a civil say to his civil question, brother?"

The office gorgio looked at the wicked thin face of him, and went green, he being perhaps forty pounds heavier than Two-Water, and some five inches taller. He licked his lips too, but differently.

"I didn't understand," he muttered. "What was the question, sir?"

Well, him and Two-Water got on very well, and the office gorgio helped Two-Water as much as he could. But it wasn't a lot in the end. Only that the place where secretaries or typists from outside would call was one special office, and a girl writer on her own wouldn't have more than five offices where she could be calling, and there hadn't been any journalist girl in on the day Two-Water mentioned.

Not a lot, but it was something. So young Smith set out to track down all the places where secretaries or typists or writers might have called in the studio. That wasn't too hard, because he was dealing with a quick, nice type of girl in all the places, and girls always liked Two-Water.

It must have been funny to the people who worked in the big block of offices attached to the studios to see Two-Water Smith trailing up the corridors and in the doors, for all the world as if he were tracking a lost horse on Dunstable Downs. But he got on all right with the girls.

"A girl of just your own height I am seeking," he told one secretary, after he had made her stand up and have his eyes run over her. "Just your height, and might be half a pound heavier. Dark brown eyes, and her arms would be muscular. Upstanding, with the weight on the front of her feet, and maybe a finger-thickness more across the shoulders than yourself. Her——" He stopped, for the girl was spluttering with laughter. Then he grinned when he saw she meant it friendly.

"Don't be a half-wit," she told him. "What way is that to describe one girl to another? What you have to look out for is things about her clothes, her lipstick and perfume, what kind of shoes and stockings, and so on. *Then* any girl will be able to answer your questions, but not with your talk about height and weight, as if you were talking about a horse."

"Your husband will be a lucky man," said Two-Water Smith. "And all his girl-friends will want to poison you. Now I will give you good luck and thanks. For my eyes saw the other things you mention—but I did not know what questions to ask. *Now*——"

And in he started, with a description of the missing girl's clothes, and stockings, and perfume, and shoes, that made the office-secretary stare. Long before he had finished she was nodding.

"Why—ye-es," she said slowly. "You must be right. What was that you said about the glove?"

"A light leather glove," repeated Two-Water at once. "It might be kid-goat, but my guess is the skin of a hare. The colour of the top of a jar of milk after standing all night. Second left finger with a tiny stain of cigarettes—a thin black kind of cigarette, not English. The smallest bit of lip-paint on the first finger of the glove, on the outside near the tip."

"Yes," said the secretary girl, without any more hesitation. "Wait a minute." She searched back through an appointment book. "Here you are. Miss Miriam Lee. Called on Mr Gronleigh last Thursday afternoon."

Two-Water thanked her and went out. There was no great difficulty about his getting a minute with Gronleigh, one of the heads, who already knew the young wagon-man by sight. But the girl was not an employee of his, nor did he know her, she being merely the secretary of a man with whom the company had business. But he was able to give Smith the man's name and address.

Then at the last minute he called Two-Water back and gave him a letter, for which Smith was grateful, as he was already beginning to find out that you couldn't get into offices without a letter, or without mention of fighting to come. So he hurried across London, to the office of Mr Theodore Carlow.

Carlow, a genial fat man, made the strange-looking visitor welcome, and after a few minutes' gossip asked what he could do. Now, Two-Water Smith had been sitting on the edge of his chair, expecting every second that the door would open and this Miriam Lee would come in, as he felt sure with the five senses of his body that he was in the right place. When Carlow said no, there was no Miss Lee a secretary there, Smith drew a long breath.

"Smaller than me by just under two inches," he explained. "Dark brown eyes. Arms with muscle to them, and a way of standing on her toes. A tint of lip-paint on one finger of the left glove—but you wouldn't know about that. Smokes thin black cigarettes—you'd know that. Uses a perfume that is clove-pink with a tinge of lily-valley—you'd know that. Uses a portable typewriter in a dark-green leather box with four little rubber feet—you'd know that. By name Lee."

Carlow was smiling at his eagerness, and reached to press a button on his desk. He motioned to Two-Water to wait, and then the door opened and a girl came in.

She was the right height, and brought a portable typewriter with her, and her eyes were brownish. But she never looked at Two-Water, only waited to see what Carlow required.

When Smith made no sign Carlow waved towards the girl.

"This is my secretary, Miss Watson," he explained. "I have no other secretary or typist." He waved to the girl, and she went out; then he turned to Two-Water again.

"Is there anything else, Mr Smith?" he inquired. "I am sorry I cannot help, and I do hope you succeed in finding your—er—your friend. Any time I can do anything——"

"That's now," said Two-Water Smith. "That's now; this minute. Who smokes the little black cigarettes in this office?"

"No one," says Carlow, smiling, and pulled out a cigar-case. "I think Miss Watson smokes Players. No one uses black cigarettes."

"You're a liar," said Two-Water quietly. "Who'd put down a typewriter with four little rubber feet, just *there*?" And he jabbed a hand at a place near Carlow's desk.

"No one," said Carlow quickly. "I mean—Miss Watson, I suppose, surely."

"You're a liar," said Two-Water again. "For hers is full half an inch narrower. Furthermore, gorgia man," he went on, and his voice was purring dangerously, "who'd use a scent of clove-pink with a touch of lily-valley?" Carlow laughed a big laugh of relief.

"Wrong, gipsy-man," he grinned. "Wrong, Sherlock Holmes from the caravan. For Miss Watson's scent is strong enough, and it——"

"I know," cut in Smith. "I smelled her. Go on."

"There isn't anyone here has ever used that perfume," said Carlow confidently. "Not for——"

"Not since last Thursday evening. Or it might be Friday morning," said Smith. "Now I will tell you a small story about my grandfather."

Carlow gaped at the sudden change in the conversation. Then after a laugh, and a glance at the clock, he relaxed and leant back in his chair.

"Do, please," he invited. "I am always interested in——"

"This grandfather of mine," said Two-Water, "was called Chip Smith, short for Chipperfield, and he was a bushranger in New South Wales, in Australia."

Carlow did not look quite so comfortable. But he managed to smile, and waited.

"The blacks," went on Two-Water, "raped and murdered a girl Chip Smith was loving, and he spent six weeks in the bush until he got the black that did it." Carlow lit a cigar, and his hand shook a little.

"He punched the black with his fists," said Smith, "for three hours, until the black was screaming with pain, and until Chip Smith was weary. Then Chip went to bed, to rest himself, after he'd chained the black to a post. Next morning he flogged him with a lizard skin until that man was a single wound from heel to neck. Then he gave him a chopper, and made him chop enough sticks to make a fire."

Carlow leant forward breathlessly, his fat face pale, and watched the lean brown man with painful intensity. Two-Water Smith rolled himself a thin black cigarette, and lit it slowly, and blew a long breath of the smoke round the room, while Carlow waited, straining.

"The right hand," said Smith quietly, "the right hand that had cut the girl's throat—Chip Smith made the black man chop the fingers off it one by one, and he made him roast them, and he made him eat them." There was a gasp from the man at the desk.

"Then," said Two-Water, "since he'd raped the girl as well, Chip Smith gelded him, before he let him go. That's all, fat man," he finished, and stood up slowly. Slowly he reached into a pocket, and whipped out a jack-knife. "Now," he hissed, "do you want to be gelded?"

Carlow's hand shot out towards the bell-push on the desk, but the jack-knife came down and pinned the hand to the wood. In a second Smith's first and second fingers, forked, were at the other's eyes, and the fat man quivered in terror.

"Speak up," ordered Two-Water. "One second after I stop

talking your eyes will be on your cheek-bones *to start with*. Now speak up."

Carlow was gabbling the story almost as soon as the other's last word was out. It was a very simple and ordinary story according to him. Miriam Lee had been his secretary. He had made a pass or two, as he put it. Smith would understand, being a man. A pass or two. The girl had never listened for a second, but had never really shown herself horrified or furious until, until——"

"Pull ahead," ordered Smith. "Until last Thursday."

"Thursday evening," agreed the other. On the Thursday evening she had returned from a secretarial job at Shepherd's Bush Studios. As she was leaving Carlow had "made a pass at her in the ordinary way," but she had repulsed him angrily. That had—he pleaded apologetically—that had worked Carlow up, and he had grabbed the girl, in the office, thrusting her back towards a couch. The fat man stopped suddenly, and gaped in terror at the wicked, weasel-like face before him.

"Pull sharp," ordered Two-Water. "What did you do to her?"

"*Me*," almost screamed Carlow. "What did *I* do. The bitch jabbed a knee in me—here—and forked her fingers at my eyes, the same as you did, and——" He gasped, and stared. Two-Water Smith was choking with laughter as he leant to jerk out the knife, and the fat man hastened to dab a handker-chief on his hand.

"P-pull ahead," gasped Smith, between laughs. "What else?"

Shamefaced, Carlow stammered out the rest of the story. He had punished the girl in the only way he knew, in a house-fashion. Her job was important to her, as he was well aware, so he had dismissed her at a moment's notice. That was all, really, and surely, Mr. Smith, as between men, would under-stand that making a pass or two meant no real harm. Nothing really, and if——"

"The address," cut in Smith curtly, and turned away to the

door when it was furnished. "Now, that's a friendly girl," he remarked pleasantly. "Just imagine what a good turn she did you, when she went to fork your lamps." He extended the first two fingers of his right hand, and Carlow shivered. "Just think what she saved you from—because you'd have looked very untidy, going round without your——" He held out the jack-knife, and bellowed laughter again, while Carlow wilted as the visitor went out.

Two-Water hurried to the Bloomsbury address, and found the brown-eyed girl cooking an egg in an upstairs room. She had stopped to call "Come in," but went on with her cooking when she saw who had arrived.

"Oh, it's you," she commented. "I thought you'd be round."

They talked for five minutes, and there was little to say. Right romani she was, and knew it, although she was born in London and her mother was born in London, and she laughed with Two-Water at poor fat Carlow's fear of the lamp-fork.

"Well, there it is, tawny one," said Plingro Lem at the end. "If you want to be my mort and come out on the road, come on. Or if you want to live in the house-town, I suppose we can do that too."

"You?" said Miriam, and stared, and laughed.

"This film lark is good money," Two-Water explained. "We can wait around easy and comfortable, and look at these nice gorgia places, until they are making the next film with my horse and wagon in. Then we have the good money again." He looked angry, for Miriam was choking with laughter.

"Twenty years," she spluttered, "or it might be thirty, before they make another Red Wagon. Are we to wait around to see if——"

"Right," said Two-Water. "My wagon's at Shepherd's Bush and they want rid of it. We can be over the Watford Bypass before evening, and pitch down by the canal at Abbot's Langley. Come on."

CHAPTER NINETEEN

The Breed of Cleopatra

MELIA CANIDOE went the road alone, in a light, small wagon with a slow, stout cob. Ninety-five, or maybe ninety-six, Melia could still steer the cob to grass and water, make her solitary camp, pass the night, and be away before sunrise, even at a summer's dawning, and long before it in winter.

She went the road alone. Because now she was the only Canidoe on the road, and she could not come, in the days of the end of her clan, to beg into the wagons of who would have her. Though many would, for Melia was well close and clan on the road, from High Strome Ferry, above the Kyles of Bute, to Hangman Crossing, on the Cornish moors.

Not just for profit either, although the tongue in her head was worth hard gold money, and Melia could talk fair gift from any satisfied gorgia, man or woman, and they loved to give it, for Melia knew words. Not just for profit, but for the friend-way, could Melia go in any wagon on the road. But her say was that the Canidoe would finish as they started, one lone woman.

The Canidoe began a long time ago, that was her say, began in the year that people first had names. Once was a time when

o

no one in England or Ireland or France had a name, only if a
man had one leg they called him One-leg, and if he had red
hair they called him Red. People were called Tom or Dick,
and that was all the name they had. Only the Canidoe, of all
the west world, had names. But it matters nothing now, for the
Canidoe clan is ending. Bury me down.

Bury me down when I die, with the gold earrings buried,
as is our way, and the high gemmed combs that were the
Queen of Spain's, and the gold wedding-ring to weigh nine
gold coins, although man was never mine and I went the road
alone. Now bury the things with me, for it is in the say.

The says are mixed now, mixed in behind my eyes, and
sometimes I will not know if it was yesterday, or back a
thousand years before the Crucifying, or on a thousand years
after it, in the days of the Galley-break, but what does it
matter now.

Yet I knew every say, for ninety years and more, and gave
the say for well seventy, because I had no man and no call from
a man, so I could go the road and give the say. But now they
are mixed, and it does not matter. Bury me down.

Only one say every one knows on the road, the say that no
Canidoe ever mated outside the Canidoe, and that their clan
and family kept to themselves. In the Greek country and in
Spain, in Ireland and England, and over in France before the
king-killing, the Canidoe kept to themselves.

Well and better it is known to all on the road that above
and beyond all were the Canidoe the right real Egypt people,
before the Feys, that were only the hired Canidoe magic-
makers, and before the Dannara-kye, that called themselves
kings in Ireland but were the gold-workers of Egypt long ago,
and made the earrings you will bury down now.

Only the romani people had names at the time of the
Galley-break, but they could not use them, for none in Ireland,
and none in England, knew what a name was. They had
no names because they had no say, and so would not need
them.

For if a man only wants to eat corn, or drink clear wine, or lie with a woman, then he has no need to give a say about that. Then if there is no say what need has he of a name? He will not need a name just to lie with a girl or drain a jug.

So in Ireland the people had no names, only nine hundred years ago, and nine hundred years is not much, in a big say, not much. Then in that country the road-people went the road, and gave their say quiet among themselves sometimes, but for the rest they were like the Irish of that day, with no more name than the greyhounds and horses.

It was like that in England too, and in all the west countries. The people had no say, and nothing to say, so they pointed to their food or drink. A man was called Tom, or Dick, or Harry, and then Tom's son would be called Thomson, and Dick's son Dickson, and Harry's son would be Harrison, and that was all. Every one knows the say.

Only the romani people had names, out of all England and Ireland and France.

Now it came on that there was a king in Ireland, and his name was Brian. He had no other name, for no one had a name then. This Brian man won a big fight, in the year the many galley-ships were broken, on the rocks of Dublin Bay and on Skerryvore, in Scotland. A gorgio he was, this Brian.

Good half of Ireland, and good half of Scotland, was tent-people and wagon-people in that day. House-towns were none or few, and the other places little more than a worth of tams, a ring of skin huts that the road-folk would scorn. But that was Ireland, in the year of the galley-wrecks, when this man Brian won the battle.

Now he was a bully kind of a man, for that was his nick-name too, Burra Brian, as a wagon-man would say, to give out that he was of the bullying kind. So the Irish, the wagon-folk and the skin-house people, they called him Brian Borra, the bully that he was. Because when he won this war he said he would be king for all the Irish now, and each man should have a house, or his head would be cut off, and each man should have a name, or he would sup sorrow for it.

Then in England they gave out a law at about the same time that every man had to have a name or it would be worse for him. And that he had better have a house, or it would be worse for him too. That was the time when the Irish, and the English, were changing over to have house-towns. Although you will see what they were from the names, and not mistaking, for you will often find a name of a town in Ireland, and in the Irish speech it means a circle of tents. Or you will find them in England, with names like Tamworth, and it means a circle of tents too, romani words and romani things.

But only some went into the towns and had names. For what should the wagon-people do, that had names already a thousand years, when some Irish gorgio or some English gorgio tells them to have a name and a house. Most had none.

But in time some borrowed and stole names from the gorgia, to pass their way and travel their road. And of one large family all borrowed names except one girl. All. Her brothers and her father, her mother and her sisters, and all the married ones that came in, they borrowed a name from the son of the Irish gorgia king. They, who had a name from the princes of Egypt, a thousand years before the Man on the Cross, a full thousand years, they took the clan name of the king's son, and went their road in safety.

Now this Brian king had this son, who had a sword-wound as a young man, so that his neck was awry. And in the days before the law to have names he had a nickname only, and was called Crooked-neck, or Crooked-neck the son of Brian. Then, for joke or for boast, who will say, when the name-law was passed by his father he took a name, as he must. But the name he took was the same, Crooked-neck, only now it was not a nickname but his own.

So that was the name this family borrowed. Crooked-neck. Many ways there are to say it, on the road among the families—Cannadine and Kennedy, Kinnedin and Carradeen and Kennedine, but they all mean the same thing, in the Irish speech, and in the Scots speech, and in other people's talk too. They mean crooked-neck.

But this lone girl with the Egypt name, she would not give up to be called Crooked-neck. So she broke with her family, and went the road alone, with five horses and a tall two-wheel yoke because there were no long wagons in Ireland. She went the road alone, with her wolfhounds and a tame eagle that could kill a man, and the black knife in her hose, and that was all.

Now, you may think, the Irish then were even worse than they are to-day, to fight and drink and rant after women. So a lone maiden going the road would be safe. She would be safe to be giving suck before nine moons were lifted, and that was sure of the Irish. But this girl with her eagle and her wolfhounds was different, although she came to think in time that no romani were left, but all had given up to the law, and taken Irish names like Crooked-neck, and gone into the skin-house towns.

So she was sad. For this girl had beauty.

Then one day she got to the coast, and there was a ship, with nine decent-looking men to man it, pirates or the like. They offered if she would go with them, and they would go to the Kyles of Bute in Scotland, for there had been a big galley-wrecking there. So she went in, and they made their way for Scotland.

Then the first night it looked like the nine of them together would come at her, but they had some small fear because she looked unlike an Irish girl, as indeed she would, coming off the road. And the minute she told them she was the daughter of a king they believed her, and by the same time when she told them her Egypt name they could not say it, but thought that Canidoe was such a name as Kennedy or Cannadine, and that she was one of the Crooked-neck king-people.

So now instead of hauling her to their bed they were to have a king's ransom, or a king's daughter's ransom, when they got back to Ireland. So they treated her well. Except for one who forgot himself one night, but she made a girl of him with the black knife and all was quiet after that. But in Scotland they tied her hands, and left her in the ship, until they would fish up the things from the wrecked galleys.

Only while they were doing that, down came some of the Fays and such people, and killed them all in quick time, and took their ship. Then what was in that ship but a girl with her hands tied.

There is no say that the Fays and the rest were much different from the Irish. But one fought with another to see who would have the girl with the hands tied. Only she called out her name and three words with it, and the fighting stopped, and the leader came to untie her hands.

Then she went with them to their worth of tams, the ash-bend tents that the Fays make still, and an old woman said she was to be Queen of Scotland. But with a single horse and the eagle and one wolf-dog she took the road, alone.

Until in the high mountains, one night while she was asleep, a man carried her off, while his dogs were fighting hers. Then the surest thing in those mountains that night was that she would be beginning her belly-swell before morning, but in boasting laugh he called out his name to her, and his name was Canidoe, the same as her own.

There is no say about how tent-people gave a marriage-say at that time in that place, but in one week they were on the road, Canidoe his wife and Canidoe her husband, and now instead of no name they had two, but they were the same name after all. So she called him Canidoe Melior, and he called her Canidoe Melia, to know one from the other. Past a hundred she was before she died, and a tall lovely woman to the end, with twenty tall sons behind her, and two daughters.

That was the beginning of the Canidoe, from one lone woman. No one on the road needs a say that we kept to ourselves. A thousand years before the Man on the Cross, and now, near a thousand years since the first giving of names, the

Canidoe keep to themselves. In Egypt, and Spain, and England, and Ireland, and France, and all the small countries in the crossing of the seas, the Canidoe never married but with the Canidoe.

Tall men and lovely women. Tall men, anyway, for it is not Melia Canidoe's say that the Canidoe women were lovely now, for there is but one Canidoe on the road, near a hundred, and none other to show. Plain say it is for every one that there was fighting with the other wagon families, all down the years, because no woman went out of her own wagons. All will know, and it is in many says.

When the Dutch king came and said that England was his, a hundred years before the gorgia killed their king in France, there came a wagon family from the Dutch country, fine men called Boschsevel, that had been left in the Dutch country a hundred years, out of Spain. And one of them wanted mating with Melia Canidoe.

Three of the Canidoe he killed, her brothers that he said were her husbands, as they said in Egypt long ago. Three of them. Then claimed Melia Canidoe, and she killed him with a knife while he reached to kiss her. None of the Bosivel-kye will mind the old say now, for they know the say of old, and Boschsevel was their kye. But the Canidoe stayed to themselves.

Down the generations the fighting went on, with fine wagon-men who would not know, and could not know, that the Canidoe must mate with Canidoe, but wanted the girls, and fought for them, and sometimes killed and sometimes died. Down the generations, but never was there any mixing.

In the year when the King of France, Napoleon that was, escaped from the gaol-island where they had put him, and went out to fight the English at Waterloo, my mother was born. Melia Canidoc, and only two families of the Canidoe in the wagons now, and only one Melior Canidoe, that was laid out to be her man, laid out to be her man before she was born, for they still kept to themselves. Count it, who can count, tally it on a stick, it is a hundred and thirty-five years since my mother came out. Melia Canidoe the last but one.

It is only a hundred and thirty-five years ago, only that time since my mother was born, and it is but short in the says, and every one will have heard them on the small heath. Every one will know that this Melia Canidoe was to mate with the only other man-Canidoe, him the only man–one of the other wagon. For they kept to themselves, as in Egypt long ago, and even when the Boschsevel killed Melia's brothers that they said were her husbands.

That say is not mixed, for it is but a hundred and thirty-five years. But the others mix themselves, until sometimes now I will not know if a man made to kiss me when I had nineteen years, or if he came eight hundred years ago when the Norman soldiers took down the names on paper, or a hundred before that when I would not have me called Crooked-neck. Only now Melia Canidoe still goes the road alone, but not with wolfhounds and an eagle now, only a lurcher and two tame jackdaws. Bury me down.

So it went down through the generations and down through the centuries, with the rake of wagons getting smaller, from thirty-five wagons at the time of the king-killing in England to bare two wagons, this and another, in the day when my mother was born, back a hundred and thirty-five years.

So there was but one man in all the world with the name on him right to mate with her. Only one. And they married.

Now what will men say of that last Melia's brood, that last but one Melia Canidoe, my mother, and I the last. Nine sons and five daughters, with me the youngest coming when she was past forty, as good men as ever backed a horse or travelled the road. As good women as ever—but no matter for that; it is no say for the last Melia of all to give out about the daughters. Bury the comb, that was the Queen of Spain's, and send my jackdaws to Mella Scampe.

For the say of the Canidoe is not mixed now. Not mixed but easy. Because there is no Canidoe clan.

Nine men and five girls in one wagon-family, the finest breed on the road. Four girls and four men in the other, the finest breed on the road. Now the Canidoe were to build the clan again, as they were in the days of Egypt. They were, and that was their say, but it was not to be.

By illness went seven, when the smallpox was sweeping all England, and three of those seven were girls from one wagon. The last one was the eldest, and had the same first name as myself, and was Melia Canidoe.

Then the old Queen that was in England gave out laws, not as bad as the Kings of Scotland gave out, but wicked enough, and one law was against travelling thieves. That meant the Queen of Spain, or the King of France, or the princes of Scotland, if they had no house but travelled the roads. It meant the princes of Egypt, if they had no house and travelled the roads. For the old Queen wanted all in houses, all, and she made her laws to force it.

Four of the Canidoe boys went in the gaol-house, and three were flogged, but nothing new was there in that say, for all who travel the roads have a say in their family like that. But Melia Canidoe went too into the storipen, into the gaol-house because she had no house, and the old Queen kept her there. And she died.

It was the end of the Canidoe clan, but not the end yet, for now I am ninety-five, or maybe more because the papers were changed in the Crimea days. Maybe more. But for me there was no man of the Canidoe, and that meant no men. So I travel the road, alone, until now, and soon it is an end.

The says are mixed, and it does not matter, for there is no child to take them along to her children. The says are mixed, and sometimes it will be Crooked-neck Brian that looks in at my wagon window, and sometimes the tawny Boschevel out of Dutchland, that I stabbed when he leant to take me—only that was an earlier Melia. Then sometimes it will be the tall tawny Canidoe, from over the Peak-hill of Derby, that was to be my man but is no man anywhere now, and he will change into that first Canidoe in the mountains of Scotland.

Only now I do not go the road with four wolfhounds and an eagle. But with one lurcher-dog and two tame jackdaws, the jackdaws that are to go to Mella Scampe. Now I will go the road, a little farther because I must, to meet the reaper by the Boricosh, and then it will be the end of the Canidoe say, and bury the combs.

CHAPTER TWENTY

Wagon-meet

ON the wide grassy downs where the Epsom Derby is run there
has always been, from the earliest days, a big rake of romani
wagons. Also away north in Lancashire, at Altcar, when the
Waterloo Cup takes place, the caravans pull in from far and near.

For hundreds of miles the wagon-clans come to Epsom, for
hundreds of miles to Altcar. At each place there will be wagons
from north and south, some having covered long distances.
But at each there will always be some missing. Altcar is a
little too far north for a caravan from Cornwall; Epsom is
perhaps too far south for the wagons from Gretna or Carlisle
or Bewcastle Fells.

In between is one big race-meeting, at Doncaster, to which
all the wagons go, from Wales and Dumfries, from Sussex
and Durham, and it is the biggest wagon-meet in Britain now.
One may see them come in, off a little road that misses the
Great North, for the Great North Road is no place for a
romani caravan.

It is a narrow road, and little used except at race times, but
it is a busy track for the wagon-people, hurrying on to cross
the great highway and get along over the quiet way to the

races. Up here they come, from the mountains of Wales and the East End of London, from the outskirts of Ipswich and the wild moors of Somerset, from the back lanes of Nottingham and from Bewcastle Fells.

Little black canvas-topped wagon, round-roofed, the canvas stretched over curved ash bends, as the tents were made in the old days—over it comes, a romani tam on wheels, and sneaks hastily across the Great North. Behind it a long painted van lumbers up on tall wheels, dwarfing the black cover-van, an opulent residence, the palace following the cottage.

One of the Lambs from Lowestoft, that could be. Their long painted wagons, carved with birds and flowers, might cost hundreds where a tam-van costs pounds, but they lumber along in line, rich and poor equal on the road.

Five long wagons push forward together, the horses urged continually, yet only barely keeping in line. Poor horses, and that means hardship somewhere. Poor wagons, one of them half painted, with new wood showing over patched scars. Sam Scampe and his clan, slowly coming up from under the crushing misfortune of their road-smash. Five wagons, with old Mella to nod and grin friendship from the last.

She has a tame jackdaw sitting with her by the window, and it is easy to know the rest of that say. Melia's earrings will be in the ground by now.

Three neat, small wagons, green-painted and with showy, shining horses, each wagon with little carved iron ornaments. Some family of the Smiths, who are all smiths, and show it in the decoration of their caravans. Two wagons behind, Smiths again, Plingro Ria and his brother this time, waving good luck and waiting the return-wish which is so important, especially on your way over to Doncaster.

One long grey wagon, with many small side-posts instead of a few heavier ones. A Dutch wagon, for that is their style. One of the Bosivels, who still ride the road in the many-ribbed caravans, although the Boschsevels their ancestors brought that style from Holland nearly three hundred years ago.

There is not much difficulty about knowing which family owns a wagon, from the shape and make of it, just as a man may know another man's name by the way he knots his diklo. Four heavy outside ribs will mean Smith or Lamb. No outside ribs, but a flat plain side, will be some Irish family. Many small wood-ribs means Bosivel, and six light wooden uprights will tell that the wagon holds Fays.

But broken ribs or shapeless wagon-sides will mean that it is Sam Scampe, or some one else who has been in a wagon-smash. Until but lately no town person could know what the words meant. An accident occurred, and a gipsy caravan was damaged. That was all. But now some people in towns know. People whose homes have been pulverized by bombs.

That is a wagon-smash.

A big yellow wagon lumbers after the Bosivels. Long roof, extending several feet past the ends of the wagon at front and rear. Carved birds flying, nearly all geese with long necks outstretched. A painted goose twirling above the stove-chimney for a weather-cock. The Brants of Essex, who have geese in their say, although they are horse-dealers and tatters and boxers.

Long, weather-beaten black wagon, with six light wooden uprights outside, drawn by a big dapple-grey. A woman at the reins, watching anxiously ahead for the danger at the Great North Road, and Torry Fay at the window, to wave good luck and wait for his own.

Seven smart wagons all close in line, horses well groomed and showily turned out, pass on to the curve and wheel out neatly, as if the road was a circus ring and the wagons were part of an act. A bright show for Doncaster, the great place for caravan-display, and these are the Herons from Surrey, owning the smartest wagons on the road.

A single beautiful wagon moves slowly, its paint gleaming as if the painting had finished only an hour earlier. The wheels are polished, even their hubs are brass, and shining. The big white horse goes high-stepping, and the harness is

costly and attractive. Some Plingro who has made money
but will not leave the road.

Two green caravans, over-long so that they look awkward,
but road-sure and well handled, pull over behind heavy black
horses. Tommity Cannadine at a window, a little older but
still Tom Sawyer, peeping eagerly for the first sight of
Doncaster.

A big piebald stallion, drawing an enormous van on high,
shining wheels, curvets and rears at the crossing, wanting to
turn back towards the mare driven by one of the Lambs. A
vast wagon, shining with mirrors and with every available inch
carved and studded, a veritable show-piece. It should belong
to the leader of leaders, the head of the Canidoe, if they
existed now.

But it is a family of the Bakers, the wagon-makers, the
craftsmen. The romani who has traded a thousand pounds in
horses, or who wins a thousand at Doncaster, may go back
down the road in that kushti vado, in that beautiful caravan,
the kushti vado of the romani songs. There it is, worth a
thousand pounds with its contents, and the Bakers make them
to sell. Some one may have luck at Doncaster, and go back
down the road in that one.

A long rake of gigs and high flats goes by, all laden with
children, the children from many families, for the caravans
keep together and the gigs keep together at this place, for
greater safety in crossing the Great North Road, the gorgia
main.

Then after the children and gigs comes a line of wagons
with lovely horses, high-stepping showily again, as if it was
part of the family pride, as indeed it is. They come on, the
burra garris, the powerful horses, what the northern romani
call the ben gries. No wonder the horses are impressive, for
behind them in the first wagon-seat is Garra Dunnaha, the man
whose very name means horseman.

Jidbell Cooper smiling from the second wagon-window,
Jidbell, who mocked the stone monuments of Cornwall.

Marly Coaper behind, the oldest and shrewdest horse-maker of them all. Then a long, bright-roofed caravan, drawn by a strong young piebald, with an ancient man smiling out for his eighty-first sight of Doncaster, smiling out at the narrow lane that used to be called the Great North Road. Old Ferra Colin from Kent, with the rest of the Colins in their flat-sided, Irish-looking vans, each one with a piebald horse like a circus show.

Brants and Bakers, Cannadines and Colins and Lambs, Jildies and Lees and Bosivels, Fays and Browns and Scampes and Herons, they pass in line, sitting alert for the road-crossing, for the passing of the gorgia main. Country people, and town people, stand in little groups by the crossing, to watch the caravans go by, and point and whisper.

And why should they not, if they like the strange spectacle? There are not too many new things to see from week to week in the towns, and the sight of the wagons is good for any eyes, but especially for eyes from a town-street.

They call, and point, as Ma Mella goes by, with the jackdaw sitting at the window beside her. And why should they not? In the towns we do not often see an old woman with a jackdaw at a window, and that room-window going the road over wheels.

They point again, and whisper, especially the girls, as Jidbell Cooper passes at her window. They point, at the lissom, healthy, attractive girl, guessing and whispering about her knowledge of horses and men. Why should they not, for the interest in such things is life, and this strange way of life has a powerful pull for the town-people.

There is no need for them to think Grania Fay romantic, but only to know her strange, and that is enough. No need, either, to give the romantic word to Black Harry Smith, smiling Black Harry, sitting carelessly sideways in his wagon-seat, holding his black mare's reins with apparent unconcern, but alert every second for the danger of the road-crossing.

There is no need for us, for house-people, to romanticize those who live above wagon-wheels. It is a way of life, strange in our eyes, although it exists side by side with our own, alien as the waters of the Nile, although it passes before us, to cross the Great North Road for Doncaster. Strange, and therefore interesting. Ancient, and therefore fascinating. Eternal, or apparently eternal, and therefore consoling to troubled eyes.

It is old life, travelling beside the new, going by with the lumber of wagon-wheels to chorus the shriek of the twentieth century down the big road. Old life, and one may watch it and be happy, without need to call it romantic.

Although even that word belongs to the romani too, in some way. By chance or not by chance, one can hardly say the word romantic without saying romani first. It has been thus for centuries, since people first began to live in western towns, and it is a good thing.

It is a good thing. That is my say.